Three Mile an Hour God

Three Mile an Hour God

Biblical Reflections

KOSUKE KOYAMA

ORBIS BOOKS
Maryknoll, New York 10545

Second Printing, November 1982

The Catholic Foreign Mission Society of America (Maryknoll) recruits and trains people for overseas missionary service. Through Orbis Books Maryknoll aims to foster the international dialogue that is essential to mission. The books published, however, reflect the opinions of their authors and are not meant to represent the official position of the society.

Library of Congress Cataloging in Publication Data

Koyama, Kosuke, 1929-
    Three mile an hour God.

    Includes bibliographical references.
    1. Meditations. I. Title.
BV4832.2.K683 1980   242   79-24785
ISBN 0-88344-473-9

Copyright © 1979 by Kosuke Koyama

First published in 1979 by SCM Press Ltd, 58 Bloomsbury Street, London WC1

U.S. edition 1980 by Orbis Books, Maryknoll, NY 10545

Phototypeset by Input Typesetting Ltd, London
Printed and bound in the United States of America

To our three teenagers
Jim in Berlin
Mimi in New York
Mark in Dunedin

Contents

Preface

In 1945 Japan was reduced to ashes. Since the war history has dealt with Japan far more kindly than she deserved. There was no North Japan and South Japan! Recovery was rapid and unrestrained. In 1978 she had a trade surplus of $24.6 billion!

I cannot see Japan today in isolation from my experience in the demonic war years, 1930–1945. The idolatry of the emperor worship brought the nation to utter destruction and inflicted enormous suffering upon her neighbours in Asia and beyond. Why is idolatry so destructive? I have lived and shall live with this question. I do not enjoy its persistent nagging. I would rather escape such 'morbid' thought and rejoice in the $24.6 billion surplus! . . . but I cannot bring myself to do so.

Why is there such total destruction? I asked in the wilderness of Tokyo. Gradually I began to see the mysterious relationship between destruction and idolatry – not only for the individual but for the life of the nation. There is no neat analysis to the question; Why is idolatry so destructive? Yet we are gripped by the problem. The question has humbled me. It has slowed me down. I have stood under the mystery of the injury that idolatry has brought upon us.

This small book is a collection of biblical reflections by one who is seeking the source of healing from the wounds, the festering sores, inflicted by the destructive power of idolatry. As he felt his way the image of the 'Three Mile an Hour God' who invites us *in the direction of depth rather than distance* has been pressed upon him.

I Life Deepening

1 Three Mile an Hour God

All the commandment which I command you this day you shall be careful to do, that you may live and multiply, and go in and possess the land which the Lord swore to give to your fathers. And you shall remember all the way which the Lord your God has led you these forty years in the wilderness, that he might humble you, testing you to know what was in your heart, whether you would keep his commandments, or not. And he humbled you and let you hunger and fed you with manna, which you did not know, nor did your fathers know; that he might make you know that man does not live by bread alone, but that man lives by everything that proceeds out of the mouth of the Lord. Your clothing did not wear out upon you, and your foot did not swell, these forty years. *Deuteronomy 8.1–4*

And Jesus went away from there and withdrew to the district of Tyre and Sidon. And behold, a Canaanite woman from that region came out and cried, 'Have mercy on me, O Lord, Son of David; my daughter is severely possessed by a demon.' But he did not answer her a word. And his disciples came and begged him, saying, 'Send her away, for she is crying after us'. He answered, 'I was sent only to the lost sheep of the house of Israel.' But she came and knelt before him, saying, 'Lord, help me.' And he answered, 'It is not fair to take the children's bread and throw it to the dogs'. She said, 'Yes, Lord, yet even the dogs eat the crumbs that fall from their master's table.' Then Jesus answered her, 'O woman, great is your faith! Be it done for you as you desire.' And her daughter was healed instantly. *Matthew 15.21–28*

God wanted to teach his people that 'man does not live by bread alone, but that man lives by everything that proceeds out of the mouth of the Lord'. This was an extremely important lesson for his people to know and understand before they went into the land of Canaan. God decided to spend forty years to teach this one lesson. Mind you, forty years for one lesson! How slow and how patient! No university can run on this basis. If God decided that he would use forty years, the subject of the lesson must be of great importance in his view. In truth we are still finding today how critically important this lesson is. Whether we agree with it or not, it seems to me that the history of mankind more or less endorses such an observation.

This lesson cannot be learned easily in a comfortable classroom.

The classroom is not free from a 'classroomish' distance from the confusing reality of life. In the classroom, theory rather than story, dominates. God's people must learn about bread and the word of God realistically and experientially. He took the people into the wilderness. The wilderness is an open space in all directions. It is a place full of possibilities. The mind can stretch out or plunge into deep meditation in the wilderness. But at the same time this open space is a dangerous, desolate space inhabited by demons and evil spirits. It is space not cultivated – not civilized. The wilderness is thus full of promise and full of danger.

Now the people of God found themselves in the wilderness. They were away from their familiar streets, grocery stores, railway stations, dentists, banks, schools, and hospitals. The familiar system and style of life were left behind. They felt increasingly precarious. The wilderness was no longer a phenomenon outside of them. Both promise and danger had come into their souls. '. . . he humbled you.' They walked in the wilderness surrounded by danger of hunger and promise of manna. Here, God taught his people, that 'man does not live by bread alone, but that man lives by everything that proceeds out of the mouth of the Lord'. The people of Israel had this experience on behalf of all of us.

Wilderness, then, is the place where we are face to face with danger and promise. And that is an educational situation for the people of God. When danger and promise come together to us, it is called crisis. The Bible does not simply speak of danger. If it did so, the biblical faith would be reduced to a 'protection-from-danger-religion'. The Bible does not simply speak about promise. If it did so, the biblical faith would be reduced to a 'happy-ending-religion'. The Bible speaks about a crisis situation, co-existence of *danger* and *promise* – wilderness – and there God teaches man. In the wilderness we are called to go beyond 'protection-from-danger-religion' and 'happy-ending-religion'. There we are called to 'trust' in God.

Let us consider for a few minutes the subject of God's lesson; 'Man does not live by bread alone, but that man lives by everything that proceeds out of the mouth of the Lord.' 'Bread' stands for the things we need. The Bible does not say, 'Man does not live by after-shave-lotion alone. . . .' Man can very well live without after-shave lotion. But bread is a different story. Man cannot live without bread. But man must not live even by this essential bread alone. Bread-alone, shelter-alone, clothing-alone, income-alone, all these *alones* damage man's quality of life. Strangely, these good values contain danger-elements too. Man is supposed to eat bread. But what if bread eats man? People are dying from over-eating today in the affluent countries. Man is supposed to live in the house. But what if the house begins to live in man? Isn't it true that we are fast forgetting the spiritual and cultural beauty of simple living? What if fashion begins to dictate to man what to wear? Would not this produce indecency and wastefulness? What if income is using man instead of man using his income? Does not this often lead man to strains and mental exhaustion? Man must not live even by all these essentials alone. Man needs the bread plus the word of God.

What a 'religious theory'! What a nervous 'religious' way to live. Bread is bread, with or without a word of God! We eat bread without theological comment. We need all kinds of essentials and non-essentials. After-shave-lotion does occupy an authentic place in our life! Why do we need the word of God over and beyond all our life's essentials and non-essentials? Perhaps we do not need it. Perhaps all by which we live can be expressed by 'bread' and 'after-shave-lotion'. But when something happens to us and we are hit by storm and we are thrown into the precariousness of the wilderness . . . should we still say that man shall live by 'bread' and 'after-shave-lotion' alone? Would we say so in the midst of the storm? Perhaps we would say so. But we would be less inclined to say so. In the wilderness our speed is slowed down until gradually we come to the speed on which we walk – *three miles an hour.*

On one of his preaching tours, Jesus walked into the district of Tyre and Sidon. He was met by a Canaanite woman. What we hear is one of the strangest stories we encounter in the gospel. We do not know much about this woman. Was she poor? Was she fairly well off? What was the size of her family? What did her husband do? Are they happy with each other? Or did they have a different sense of values in their everyday engagement? Are they communicating with their children well? We don't know. But we do know that this woman was hit by a storm.

She 'came out and cried, "Have mercy on me, O Lord, Son of David; my daughter is severely possessed by a demon".' It is not that someone next door is possessed by a demon, but my daughter. It is not that my daughter once a year suffers possession by a demon. She is severely possessed by a demon. She is exposed to naked threat and danger. How agonizing! Her whole life is now focused on her daughter who suffers. She comes to Jesus believing that she will hear the word of promise in the midst of the danger that is threatening the destruction of her daughter. Strangely, Jesus 'did not answer her a word'. Can we imagine this? With this cold silence, was not the Canaanite woman taken even deeper into the wilderness where both danger and promise intensify themselves? Read further: 'And his disciples came and begged him, saying,

"Send her away, for she is crying to us".' She is making a wilderness
scene right here on the civilized street. True, this woman is literally
sandwiched between danger and promise. She is in the wilderness.
And here she is clambering after the word of God. . . .

But let's hear more about this woman. Then Jesus spoke. Certainly it must be the word of comfort and healing? 'I was sent only
to the lost sheep of the house of Israel.' What a word! Incredibly
disappointing word for the agonizing mother! In effect Jesus said
that he is primarily responsible to the people of Israel and not the
gentile people like this Canaanite woman. Did she not believe that
the 'Lord, Son of David' was the one who would willingly show his
mercy upon her if she cried to him? She did not give up. She did
not rebel. 'She came and knelt before him, saying, "Lord, help
me".' What a great commitment to Jesus Christ. Why did not she
start looking around to find other possible help? Jesus answered –
Yes, he did! 'It is not fair to take the children's bread and throw it
to the dogs.' We all would give up at this point. What a cruel thing
to say to a woman who was 'hit by a great storm'. But hear what
this Canaanite woman said; 'Yes, Lord, yet even the dogs eat the
crumbs that fall from their master's table'.

Jesus was deeply moved. 'O woman, great is your faith! Be it
done for you as you desire.'

But what is the matter with Jesus Christ? Why did he not willingly and quickly grant her desire as he did on other occasions?
Could he not see at once the faith she had in him? Perhaps Jesus
decided to take her into the depth of wilderness so that she may
experience the promise of God more deeply and intensively than
others. She came out on the other side of 'protection-from-danger-
religion' and 'happy-ending-religion'. She trusted in Jesus Christ.
'O woman, great is your faith!' The ending of this story is not a
'happy-end'. It is a 'trust-end'. There is a vast difference between
'happy-end-religion' and 'trust-end-faith'.

We live today an efficient and speedy life. We are surrounded by
electric switches, some of which cost us 10 dollars and others may
even cost 2,000 dollars. We want more switches. Who among us
dislikes efficiency and a smooth-going comfortable life? University
students use the Xerox machine in their studies. Housewives use
'instant pizza' for supper. Men's legs are fast deteriorating from the
lack of the most basic human exercise, walking. Automobiles speed-
ing at fifty miles an hour have replaced their legs. We believe in
efficiency. Let's not just look at this negatively. There is a great
value in efficiency and speed.

But let me make one observation. I find that God goes 'slowly'
in his educational process of man. 'Forty years in the wilderness'

points to his basic educational philosophy. Forty years of national migration through the wilderness, three generations of the united monarchy (Saul, David, Solomon), nineteen kings of Israel (up to 722 BC)and twenty kings of Judah (up to 587 BC), the hosts of the prophets and priests, the experience of exile and restoration – isn't this rather a slow and costly way for God to let his people know the covenant relationship between God and man?

Jesus Christ came. He walked towards the 'full stop'. He lost his mobility. He was nailed down! He is not even at three miles an hour as we walk. He is not moving. 'Full stop'! What can be slower than 'full stop' – 'nailed down'? At this point of 'full stop', the apostolic church proclaims that the love of God to man is ultimately and fully revealed. God walks 'slowly' because he is love. If he is not love he would have gone much faster. Love has its speed. It is an inner speed. It is a spiritual speed. It is a different kind of speed from the technological speed to which we are accustomed. It is 'slow' yet it is lord over all other speeds since it is the speed of love. It goes on in the depth of our life, whether we notice or not, whether we are currently hit by storm or not, at three miles an hour. It is the speed we walk and therefore it is the speed the love of God walks.

The people of God were taught the truth of bread and the word of God in the wilderness as they walked three miles an hour by the three mile an hour God. The Canaanite woman believed in Jesus Christ against all her own speeds by trusting the speed of the promise of God.

2   Appreciation-Perspective

And they came, bringing to him a paralytic carried by four men. And when they could not get near him because of the crowd, they removed the roof above him; and when they had made an opening, they let down the pallet on which the paralytic lay. And when Jesus saw their faith, he said to the paralytic, 'My son, your sins are forgiven.'   *Mark 2.3–5*

I don't know whether Capernaum on that day was a sunny day with a clear blue sky, but certainly the friendly act of the four who helped this paralytic man brightens and warms the mind of anyone

who reads it. They wanted to bring the sick man to Jesus. They
engaged themselves in a situational technological undertaking. They
planned and decided to approach Jesus vertically. ('We are afflicted
in every way, but not crushed; perplexed, but not driven to despair
. . .' II Cor. 4.8) Obviously they were not concerned about what
the Capernaum Insurance Company would say to such an unusual
operation. The four broke through the barrier of technological and
financial walls and came straight to Jesus, the Word, who judges
technological and financial words.

Strength is creative when it expresses itself by making the weak
strong.

Precariously they let down the pallet on which the paralytic lay.
The sick man was a weak person. The strength of the four became
a healing reality when it was used to help the weak. Strength that
shows its power directly without reference to strengthening the weak
is pagan. Such demonic strength is in evidence, for instance, in the
decision of the superpowers at Vladivostok in 1975 to 'restrict'
themselves to having not more than 2400 nuclear warheads posed
to each other. Beauty is beauty when it makes not-beautiful beautiful. Rich is rich when it makes poor rich. 'For you know the grace
of our Lord Jesus Christ, that though he was rich, yet for your sake
he became poor, so that by his poverty you might become rich' (II
Cor. 8.9). Theological language is 'transitive'. Our God is a 'transitive' God, the God of the covenant-relationship. The strength of
the four friends, expressed through the act of helping the paralytic,
is a Christianized strength. It is a 'baptized' strength. The strength
here served the commandment; 'You shall love your neighbour as
yourself'. It became 'neighbourly strength'. It became 'community-
strength'.

'Jesus saw their faith.' I understand this to mean first of all that
Jesus was moved. He appreciated the 'community-strength'. He
appreciated the act of the four men and the attitude of trust on the
part of the paralytic to whatever the four men were doing for him.
All came together to Jesus. This may have seemed a small
insignificant event which took place on one of Jesus' preaching
tours. Yet it moved the Son of God. Others saw a big hole in the
roof, and the poor paralytic being let down. Jesus saw their faith. . . .
Of course, Jesus saw the hole on the roof too. The hole became the
sign of faith for Jesus. He saw their spiritual commitment in this
undertaking.

The gospel stories narrate numerous occasions in which acts of
faith moved Jesus. He was deeply moved, also, by a Canaanite
woman who believed in Jesus against all odds and insults. 'O
woman, great is your faith! Be it done for you as you desire' (Matt.

15.21–28). A centurion came to Jesus in Capernaum: ' "Lord, I am
not worthy to have you come under my roof; but only say the word,
and my servant will be healed" . . . When Jesus heard him, he
marvelled and said to those who followed him. "Truly, I say to you,
not even in Israel have I found such faith. . . .'" (Matt. 8.5–13).
'And he sat down opposite the treasury, and watched the multitude
putting money into the treasury. . . . And a poor widow came, and
put in two copper coins, which make a penny. And he called his
disciples to him, and said to them, "Truly, I say to you, this poor
widow has put in more than all those who are contributing to the
treasury . . . she out of her poverty has put in everything she had,
her whole living" ' (Mark 12.41–44). He must have been deeply
moved by this widow. 'A man ran up and knelt before him, and
asked him, "Good Teacher, what must I do to inherit eternal life?"
. . . "You know the commandments: Do not kill, do not commit
adultery," . . . "Teacher all these I have observed from my youth."
And Jesus looking upon him loved him' (Mark 10.17–22).

Jesus Christ appreciates. His mind is not destructive but
appreciative.

He appreciates man's expression of love and faith no matter how
fragmentary and momentary they are. He understands our love and
faith far better than we understand them. I cannot utter a verdict
whether these four men fulfilled God's commandment 'you shall
love your neighbour as yourself' – which is the 'whole law' (Gal.
5.14) – or not. But I know that Jesus was moved by what was done
by these four men. They must have acted in a way pleasing to God.
What else does fulfilment mean than to do a kind of act which
moves Jesus Christ, the Son of God?

While Jesus Christ, the head of the church, has an appreciative
mind, often his historical churches have displayed a non-appreciative
or even anti-appreciative mind. Only rarely is the church
moved. Often it has rejected, 'thrown cold water upon' the one who
said 'all these I have observed from my youth'. The cultural values
of Asia and the Pacific have not been appreciated. They were, in a
package, decided to be against the values for which Jesus Christ
stood, though in most cases such judgment has been given in terms
of the values found in the Western life-style for which Jesus Christ
does not necessarily stand. That which was unfamiliar to the church
was condemned as anti-Christian. One of the few most critical
problems posed to the life in the Christian faith is this lack of
appreciation-perspective.

I think the basic reason for the lack of the appreciation-perspective
in any human situation, including that of the Christian church,
is and must be absence of love. One cannot appreciate all kinds of

human relationship without having love. Love is an inner energy of
man which makes him perceptive to the presence of good and bad
in human relationships. And love is committed to encourage the
good and discourage the bad to grow anywhere. It is the mind of
God at work. So often the New Testament writers write; 'And
immediately Jesus, perceiving in his spirit that they thus questioned
within themselves, . . .' (Mark 2.8). Jesus was not a magician. He
is perceptive to what is going on in the hearts of men because he
loves them.

Jesus 'saw their faith'. They might not have seen their own faith.
That is quite possible. But Jesus saw it. He was moved. His love
expressed itself as an open declaration of 'forgiveness of sins'. Love
cannot settle down unless it heals. The love that does not heal is
not love. This appreciation-perspective, within the greater context
of love and forgiveness is the context in which we must examine
our life. In this context we are freed from merely looking at the
'hole in the roof'. We will be led to see something more.

3   New Life, an Overwhelmed Life

An when he came up out of the water, immediately he saw the heavens
opened and the Spirit descending upon him like a dove; and a voice came
from heaven, 'Thou art my beloved Son; with thee I am well pleased.' The
Spirit immediately drove him out into the wilderness. And he was in the
wilderness forty days, tempted by Satan; and he was with the wild beasts;
and the angels ministered to him.   *Mark 1. 10–13*

After one cycle of 365 days comes a new year. The image of a circle
is attractive to us. The circle is endless and gives us the impression
of being patient. It does not confront us. It embraces us. Embraced
we feel not pressured by time and thus shielded from going to the
breaking point. The shape of the mother's womb is not a cube, but
round. The great Mekong River, a water way of mother nature,
draws a magnificent circular form as it runs towards the South
China Sea. The metropolitan section of Tokyo has a loop train. In
rush hour if you could not reach the door to step down just wait for
the next round, we will come to the same station again. The circle

gives you many chances. The circle is an image of 'many times' and not of 'once for all'. Do not despair!

Our life is full of repetitions. We eat breakfast 365 times a year. We sleep 365 times a year. Repetition is a part of a circle. As we repeat we form a mental image of the circle. Repetition and circle both give us a basic sense of security. We know that winter will be followed by spring. If it were possible that winter might be followed by autumn, failing the joy of spring and growth of summer, such thought will make us insecure. If we had no sure hope of morning and high noon after the night, how should we survive? Yet repetition and circling also make us bored and sleepy. Routine may rob us of the adventures of life, ask any housewife. The merry-go-around is fun because you know you can get off from it five minutes later.

New Year is a part of this cycle. But at new year time we desire to take a distance from the flow of cycle and try to begin our time anew. It is, therefore, a time of 'rebellion' against the cycle. We want to find a new point of departure. Almost everywhere the new year festival includes some symbolic act of expulsion of demons and diseases. According to the Buddhist tradition man is afflicted with 108 kinds of greed (*klesa*). From the midnight of 31 December the temple bell will strike 108 times in Japan. As you hear each gong, you are asked to get rid of your greed one by one in preparation for the new point of departure, the new year. By cleansing yourself in this manner you are going back to the 'original purity' . . . to start again.

The important word here is *new*. We speak of a new car, new hospital, new idea and so on. *New* means a time of expulsion of demons and diseases. When demons and diseases are expelled we feel our life recreated and made *new*. This is the meaning of *new* which is hidden, for instance, when we say a new car. New car is free from the 'demons and diseases' that the old engine had. The concept of new is related to the sense of 'expulsion of demons and diseases'. It is a moment of personal enrichment, meaning and salvation.

'Thou art my beloved Son, with thee I am well pleased.' These are the words with which God introduced Jesus to the whole world. They are the words of powerful affirmation. God affirms Jesus. Jesus hears these words. He hears these words for our sake. He hears these words as our representative. With these affirming words he walks into the beginning of his ministry.

Overwhelming affirmation. God in Christ tells us that God is happy with us. Overwhelmed by such affirmation we experience *newness* in our life. To be made new is to be overwhelmed by the affirmation of God. The New Testament means the 'Affirming

Words that Overwhelm us'. When we are thus overwhelmed, be it in June or October, it is *new* year in the deeper sense. The words of overwhelming affirmation will cast out demons and diseases. 'But if it is by the finger of God that I cast out demons then the kingdom of God has come upon you ' (Luke 11.20). Don't settle down with the 108 strikes of the temple gong. Go beyond and hear the over-whelming affirmation of God if you want to experience *newness*. When God affirms our life we are made free from demons and diseases.

With the words of affirmation Jesus goes into his ministry. Into his ministry? 'The Spirit immediately drove him out into the wilder-ness.' The experience of the overwhelming affirmation is immedi-ately followed by the scene of the wilderness. Wilderness stands for precariousness and danger. It is the place where demons inhabit. But it signifies possibility and promise. In wilderness danger and promise come together to us. The affirmed life must not become either a lazy life or a happy-ever-after, easy life. The affirmed life is not a life of the power of positive thinking. To be affirmed by God means to live with danger and promise. 'None of us lives to himself, and none of us dies to himself. If we live, we live to the Lord, and if we die, we die to the Lord; so then, whether we live or whether we die, we are the Lord's' (Rom. 14.7–8). We are the Lord's. On this basis we live the life of danger and promise. We do not live and die for ourselves. Our life must not be one of isolation and egocentricity. Our life must be one of sharing.

The affirmed life is new life.
The new life is overwhelmed life.
Overwhelmed life lives with danger and promise.

4   I Cannot Push Time Around

But seek first his kingdom and his righteousness, and all these things shall
be yours as well.   *Matthew 6.33*

I see a towering pine tree in the park on my way to the university. 'Good morning. . . . If you were in the compound of a Shinto temple no doubt you would be worshipped as a sacred tree. But . . . in New

Zealand people do not do that kind of interesting thing!'

I have a special feeling about the pine tree. What is it that moves mysteriously within my soul when I see this tree? What is it that my inner ear hears when the wind rumbles through the branches? What do these pine cones speak to me when I pick them up? Why is it that I feel I want to touch the pine tree? Am I trying to receive its 'supernatural power' (*mana*)? Do I have this strange sensation about the pine tree because I am Japanese? One spot of the trunk I touch every morning as I pass. There are commuters in Tokyo who do this. On the way to the railway stations, they touch . . . it may be a roadside postbox, a telephone pole, the edge of a table of a vegetable stall. If they fail to do so they do not feel well that day. I touched this morning the same spot of this great tree and I feel assured.

I touched the tree this morning. Now I am released until tomorrow. Between today and tomorrow – until I touch you again – time flows away without my pushing it. A coffee cup will not go away unless I push it away. An oxcart will stay unless the ox pulls it away. A jumbo jet will not fly until the powerful engines propel it. But time slips away without the aid of anyone or anything. How strange! Time makes me feel as though I were not important. How important I feel when I push something or someone. Saul (later the apostle Paul), with the letter of authority from the high priest in his hands, arrested Christians (Acts 9.1,2). Arresting is an intense form of pushing. He must have felt a strong sense of self-importance. Is not pushing a physical expression of inner self-importance? The more one pushes the more one feels important. I realized this suddenly when I was pushing my way into the crowded rush hour train in Tokyo. There is a strange sense of satisfaction in pushing others. The sense of satisfaction must be related to a sense of self-importance.

But time humiliates me. It limits me. I cannot push it. Time pushes me. I say innocently that 'time flows'. Actually it may be I that am flowing. If, then, I flow, I hope to flow with time and in time. It would be intolerably lonely to be outside of time. Timelessness would be homelessness. I don't want to be orphaned by time. When I think about time I have no other choice than to be humble.

Nirvana (from the verb nibbati 'to cool by blowing') is the highest good of Buddhism. It is the state of absolute tranquility that comes to one who is completely cooled.

For him who is attached, there is vacillation; for him who is not attached, there is no vacillation. When there is no vacillation, there is calm; when there is calm, there is no delight; when there is no delight, there is not coming-and-going (i.e., continuous birth and death); when there is no coming-and-going, there is no disappearance-and-appearance; when there is no disappearance-and-appearance, there is nothing here nor there or between them; this indeed is the end of suffering. (*The Udana, Inspiring Words of the Buddha*)

This is *nirvana*, the cooled man in the cooled situation. To be cool is to be tranquil. Coolness comes to man when he frees himself from attachment. Attachment produces a 'hot' man and a 'hot' situation. When a man is attached to a colour television set and wishes to purchase it (NZ $1,000) he will find himself getting 'hot'. From this attachment a series of *hots* will follow. He must pay $600 as his first instalment. Then the rest $400 must be paid within eighteen months with interest. Eighteen months of 'hot season'! Suppose he has a similar arrangement with his car. Then the hot-season will be doubled and tripled. A great deal of sweating. Attachment is the source of disturbance. Eliminate attachment and you are cooled as the flame of a candle is blown out. Hotness is anti-tranquil. It is damnation. Coolness is tranquil. It is salvation.

. . . . I hear the Buddha speaking to us. . . . Why don't you get rid of *tanha* (thirsting greed)? When you are free from thirsting greed (excessive greed, uncontrolled self-importance) you will begin to have a distance from 'hotness'. Distance from heat is distance from the paralysing effects of time, namely, old age, sickness and death. For the cooled man, time also is cooled. Cooled time is tranquil. For the hot man time is hot. Hot time is violent. Freedom from greed is freedom from time. In reverse, closeness to thirsting greed is closeness to the effects of time. The more you thirst after yourself the stronger the grip of time upon you. Thirst after yourself? Yes. All sorts of thirsting after self-importance. I perceive . . . I may be wrong . . . in the message of the Buddha subtle suggestions of a relationship between *greed* and *time*. Time will be destructively at work upon the hot man of greedy self-importance. But time will be *nirvanic* (cooling) to those who are free from thirsting after self-importance.

I must admit that this is an unfamiliar thought to me. Greed is greed, and time is time. They seem to me to be two independent subjects. But the Buddha seems to be combining them. My greed will dictate my relationship with time. I would use my time selfishly. By using time selfishly I become progressively more selfish. The selfish use of time will bring *spiritual* destruction (age, sickness and death) to me. I experience this to be true. Somehow selfish time is destructive. I cannot explain why it is. Selfish or not selfish I shall get old, sick and die. But . . . there must be a possibility that I can get old, sick and die, yet remain spiritually hopeful, meaningful and creative. I think so. I hope so.

How can I be not selfish? Must I abandon all concern about myself? Totally? That would be plainly impossible. But I must be able to abandon *thirsting* after self-importance. I must be able to control my excessive selfishness. I should be able to distinguish between sickly selfishness and healthy self-knowledge. I sense that the total eradication of selfishness is difficult. Only a few 'religious virtuosi' (Max Weber) complete such a feat. Self-knowledge, far more creative than radical self-effacement or destruction of self, is what I must seek.

I touch my tree. Am I touching time, as day by day I relate myself once more to this constant physical reality? I want to live a life humbled by time. Touching my tree, day after day, reminds me of time. It tells me that I can only wait for time. I cannot push it or hold it. Between today and tomorrow when I touch my tree again, I can accept only those opportunities that come to create a new non-thirsting, less greedy, relationship with others and with things.

My Master said, I remember, seek the kingdom and all shall be added. He did not say to seek all these things and the kingdom shall be mine.

5 Human Spirit and Increase

And he said to them, 'Take heed, and beware of all covetousness; for a man's life does not consist in the abundance of his possessions.' And he told them a parable, saying, 'The land of a rich man brought forth plentifully; and he thought to himself, "What shall I do, for I have nowhere to store my crops?" And he said, "I will do this: I will pull down my barns, and build larger ones; and there I will store all my grain and my goods. And I will say to my soul, Soul, you have ample goods laid up for many years; take your ease, eat, drink, be merry". But God said to him, "Fool! This night your soul is required of you; and the things you have prepared, whose will they be?" So is he who lays up treasure for himself, and is not rich toward God.'   *Luke 12.15–21*

Here is a standard success story of a rich man. 'The land of a rich man brought forth plentifully.' Fertile land and hard work. In another story the lost son (Luke 15.11–32) is brought to his senses by his great hunger and despair. Deprivation made him to say 'What shall I do?' In the present parable, saturation is making the man to say 'What shall I do?' The two contexts are very different; saturation and deprivation. Yet both are asking the question with regards to the fundamental orientation of life. What shall I do? I have too little. I have too much.

The rich man is again resourceful. He plans a development programme. What he proposes to do is both efficient and acceptable. Build bigger barns. More barns. Who among us with any business sense would do otherwise? His solution is pleasing to himself. Is not this evident in jubilant words of self-congratulation? 'Soul, you have ample goods laid up for many years; take your ease, eat, drink, be merry.' His development programme is focused on himself. He aims to enlarge himself. He wants his *inside*, his soul, to be secure and enlarged. His bigger barns point to his bigger soul. He accelerates himself. He is now surrounded by security. He is a lucky man in his own estimation. His friends also accept his own estimation of himself. He is well established. He can afford to be carefree! Who among us would not envy him?

'The land of a rich man brought forth plentifully.' The great harvest has influence upon the soul. His stomach *and* soul feel much better now. They feel secure. Great harvest means a pleasing distance from precariousness and insecurity. . . . And is not a great harvest a sign of God's favour? Is not God on your side? He must be . . . Then there is a 'theological reason' to be merry, eat and drink! Can there be any situation in which man can be happier than this? God is on your side, and in his name both your soul and stomach are safe!

But we know another kind of people, the 'spiritual man'. He cultivates his inner field and 'brings forth plentifully' too. The parable of Jesus about the Pharisee and the publican (Luke 18.9–14) tells us quite frankly about such a case. 'Two men went up into the temple to pray, one a Pharisee and the other a tax collector. The Pharisee stood and prayed thus with himself, "God, I thank thee that I am not like other men, extortioners, unjust, adulterers, or even like this tax collector, I fast twice a week, I give tithes of all that I get" : . .' The Pharisee's religious field brought forth plentifully. These words of prayer are really directed to his soul. They are saying, in the religious language of the Pharisees, the same thing that the rich farmer said to himself. 'Soul, you have ample goods laid up for many years; take your ease, eat, drink, be merry.' The spiritual man speaks religious language, yet what is said can be quite irreligious. Secular people often have a sharper insight into this subtle relationship between the two languages than church people. Perhaps far more than we would accept, our spiritual life is in the line of the rich farmer. Sometimes the spiritual men get together and form powerful 'spiritual groups'. In the name of spiritual value they can raise substantial sums of money. The huge money is used for their temple building. The last thirty years witnessed a boom of temple-building in Japan and the United States for instance. The gospel of John introduces Jesus as the one who 'tented' among us (John 1.14) but now he is expensively 'templed'. . . . 'Soul, you have a beautiful temple built, take your ease, eat, drink, be merry!'

The spiritual man is, strangely, often a man of insensitivity. This is demonstrated in the attitude of the Pharisee who went up to the temple to pray. Why does a man become insensitive when he thinks about his own achievement in the temple? The temple stands for a time and place in which man is invited to experience the glory of God, not the glory of man. But it is in the temple we engage in thought of self-glorification. This is the source of the insensitivity of the spiritual man. In December 1978 there was a Billy Graham Crusade in Singapore. Massive and efficient preparation was made. The crusade was held in Singapore Sports Stadium. The city has a sizeable Muslim population with mosques. For them the term 'crusade' carries bitter historical memories of the medieval Christian crusade against the Muslims. . . . May I say I feel an absence of sensitivity on the part of the crusading Christians.

'Soul, you have ample goods laid up for many years; take your ease, eat, drink, be merry.' But, . . . it is not quite so. 'This night your soul is required of you.' This man must be perceptive enough to think of such a deadly possibility that he may get a heart attack 'this night'. Yes. I think so. He is a resourceful man. He is reasonable. He is not a fool. Having reached the point of saturation his problem is now how to enjoy this saturation. And it is more difficult than he thought. Here comes up a fundamental problem. Saturation can be enjoyed only when there is one who enjoys it. He must have thought, 'The end of my life may come to me at any moment!' None of us is free from this inevitability. And this is the thought that matures us. The Prince Shotoku of Japan (574–622) who was very actively involved in the introduction of Buddhism to Japan has been famous through the centuries for the brief sentence; *Seken Koke, Yui Butsu Zeshin* or 'This World is without Substance, Only

the World of the Buddha is True'. This saying is not unrelated to
the biblical warning we read in the parable. At every moment of
life there is the possibility of dying. . . . 'this night. . .'. And it is this
thought that matures us.

If I were to live for 2500 years like a Giant Sequoia in California
or if I were certain when the end will come to me, then I must
reorganize the whole structure of my life in order to make it somehow meaningful. I am not sure whether I could do such a reorganization. It would be far beyond my faculty of imagination and
experience of life. I am not sure that I would prefer the Giant
Sequoia life to the precarious one in which I live. We do not choose
to be precarious and transient. Yet apart from this limitation how
one can appreciate the meaning of one's life? Is not limitation
meaningful?

When limitation is devalued civilization tends to become idolatrous. There is some correlation between 'dislike of limitation' and
idolatry. ' . . . I will pull down my barns, and build larger ones. . .'

'This night your soul is required of you.' As I have suggested this
thought first must have come to him from himself. The great harvest
made him indeed secure. He was indeed jubilant. But exactly at
that moment, he became insecure and apprehensive. How strange.
He began to ask a question of the ultimate character; his own death,
his complete disappearance from this world, and his complete non-
relationship with all he has accumulated. It is a terribly disturbing
question that came to him while he is seemingly triumphant. And
. . . this is indeed the question that came from God. It goes back all
the way to the question God asked Adam and Eve in the garden,
'Where are you?' (Gen. 3.9).

The question 'Where are you?' is behind this; 'This night your
soul is required of you'. Then this is not just a warning. It is more.
It is the word that educates us. It is the word of education of
mankind rather than that of condemnation. 'The truth will make
you free' (John 8.32). The untruth will make us unfree. 'This night
your soul is required of you.' This is the word of truth, therefore,
it has power to free us. 'You must answer me,' God is saying 'where
you are!' Where do you stand with the truth that will make you
free? . . .'I will pull down my barns, and build larger ones . . .' Fine,
but do it with the good understanding that 'this night your soul is
required of you'. Then, your development programme will be a
meaningful one. It will have profound effect upon you and your
community. . . . Otherwise, you are, in spite of all your brilliant
performance, a 'fool'! Fool? Yes, not in the eyes of man, but in the
eyes of God.

The rich farmer is successful. But he is nervous. He seems to be asking a question; 'I have bigger barns and correspondingly a bigger soul. But do I love myself? To be exact, do I love myself in the right way? . . . there is something that makes me nervous. Am I possibly loving myself in the wrong way? . . .'

The parable intends to show that the rich man did not love himself in the way love is understood in the presence of God. When we speak of loving ourselves most likely we are loving ourselves wrongly. We are hurting ourselves. Our problem is how to know which love is wrong self-love and which right self-love. When do I love myself rightly? When do I love myself without incurring injury to myself and to my neighbour?

The prodigal son came home with a prepared speech. He knew that he was going to face the most critical moment of his life. His father accepted him. 'For this son of mine was dead, but now he is alive; he was lost, but now he has been found.' When the son was kissed he was restored to the dignity of humanity. There he was given again the perspective with which to look at himself. He found himself. He understood that the most profound thing he could say about himself was exactly what his father had said about him; 'I was dead but now I am alive; I was lost, but now I have been found'. This was not a monologue. It was a response to the utterance of the father's acceptance. In this response, to his own amazement, he became a new man. The response, not his prepared speech, was decisive to his resurrection.

When do I love myself without incurring injury to myself and to my neighbour? What a difficult question to answer. All of us are captivated by the power of self-love. The self-love which does not understand the relationship between 'the soul' and 'the bigger barns' will eventually injure us. The self-love which does not hear the warning of God will eventually destroy us. Self-love that integrates the mind of God is a self-love in the process of being purified. Perhaps here we may begin to love ourselves without injuring ourselves and others.

The great harvest (increase) puts the farmer in a crisis. 'Increase' is a great subject of our day. Man walks at three miles an hour. This speed can be increased if man gets in a jet plane. The passenger jet planes can fly six hundred miles an hour. In the areas of communication, transportation, education, medicine, government and finance we are noticing 'increase' in speed, volume, possession and efficiency. But so far the increase for one is only producing decrease for someone else. The world is divided into two sections; the section with many bigger barns and the section without even small barns, 'increased section' and 'decreased section'.

What does the parable of the rich farmer say to us today?

6   What is Unclean Spirit?

The sabbath was made for man, not man for the sabbath; so the Son of
man is lord even of the sabbath.   *Mark 2.27,28*

Sabbath is a time of celebration to remember the mighty saving
work of God. The well-known Genesis 2.2–3 speaks of the creation-
sabbath. 'And on the seventh day God finished his work which he
had done and he rested on the seventh day from all his work which
he had done. So God blessed the seventh day and hallowed it,
because on it God rested from all his work which he had done in
creation.' Here the verb 'rested' is the basis of the noun sabbath.
Deuteronomy 5.12–15 speaks of the exodus-sabbath; '. . . but the
seventh day is a sabbath to the Lord your God; in it you shall not
do any work, you, or your son, . . . you shall remember that you
were a servant in the land of Egypt, and the Lord your God brought
you out thence with a mighty hand and an outstretched arm; therefore the Lord your God commanded you to keep the sabbath day.'
    The sabbath is a holy institution. It expresses the sense of grati-
tude to the God of creation and exodus. It is, then, a day of rest
and joy (Isa. 1.13; Hos. 2.13). But this sign of salvation in the
covenant community gradually came to receive an unduly narrow
interpretation. Under its banner Jesus was criticized for telling a
man on the sabbath to carry his bed (John 5.10) for healing the
sick (Luke 13.14) and for plucking ears of corn (Matt. 12.2). It was
unlawful to walk more than two thousand paces (Acts 1.12). Jesus
respected the sabbath. But he rejected the interpretation and use of
the sabbath which did not mirror the mind of the creation and
exodus God. 'The sabbath was made for man, not man for the
sabbath' is fundamental if we are to keep the sabbath an occasion
of rest and joy before the God of creation and exodus.
    But Jesus was speaking of more than the sabbath. Replace the
word sabbath in this saying of Jesus with the following words;
technology, computer, money, sex, clothing, house, salary, race,
state and religion. Sex was made for man, not man for sex, race
was made for man, not man for race, and state was made for man,
not man for state. If this order were reversed, we would have
tyranny of sex, race or state which we call sexism, racism and
totalitarianism. For 'man to be made for race, not race for man'
would be preposterous. This is an unholy and unclean thought.
This preposterousness is the structure of uncleanness. If a bicycle

rides man, it is comical. But if race 'rides' man, as it were, it is unholy.

This reverse order is unholy since it destroys the order which is in accordance with the mind of the creation and exodus God. Such thought as 'man was made for house, not house for man' will eventually paralyse man.

Paradoxically this paralysis has symptoms of being 'violently busy'. 'Night and day (non-stop!) among the tombs and on the mountains he was (one who is possessed by the unclean spirit) always crying out, and bruising himself with stone' (Mark 5.5). The preposterous arrangement produces strong 'ideologies' and man becomes so dedicated to it, working 'night and day' and ignoring the primeval order set by the Creator (Gen. 1.5). '. . . but the chains he wrenched apart and the fetters he broke in pieces' (Mark 5.4). Preposterousness makes man demonically powerful. How tragic.

The man possessed by the unclean spirit must be healed. His full humanity must be restored to him. Jesus Christ, the Clean Spirit, restores to this man the right relationship with himself, his neighbours and his God. Now he is 'sitting there, clothed and in his right mind' (Mark 5.15). 'The Son of man' is 'lord even of the sabbath' because he understands and practises the clean-spirit-perspective with regards to all kinds of human institutions. He has the power to make preposterous human undertakings 'sit down, clothed and in the right mind'. Jesus Christ is, in his personality and work, the full reflection of the saving intention of the creation and exodus God.

7 Holiness – Deep, Pervading and Focusing

In the year that King Uzziah died I saw the Lord sitting upon a throne, high and lifted up; and his train filled the temple. Above him stood the seraphim; each had six wings: with two he covered his face, and with two he covered his feet, and with two he flew. And one called to another and said;

'Holy, holy, holy is the
Lord of hosts; the whole
earth is full of his glory.'

Isaiah 6.1–3

Do you ever hear the word 'holy' spoken in our society? I find it only rarely written or spoken in our newspapers, radio programmes or everyday conversation. In July 1976, there were nationwide debates over whether New Zealand's rugby team should go to the Republic of South Africa to play or not; 'no, in the name of humanity! yes, in the name of sportsmanship!' In all the discussions never once was the word 'holy' mentioned. In the critical labour dispute of New Zealand's number one industry, the freezing works, the word has not appeared. Instead 'travel-allowance' dominated the discussion. Among today's continuous waves of advertisements we do not find this word used. I have not heard 'holy deodorant' or 'holy fried chicken' advertised. We do not meet 'His Holiness' in our daily life either. There are of course words such as Holy Bible, Holy Bread, Holy Land, Holy See, Holy Scripture, Holy Sepulcher, Holy Matrimony. . . But these appear only in the special religious context. We can manage our everyday life without using this word at all. The word 'holy' has an almost esoteric sound in our 'secular' environment. I would like to attempt some paragraphs here in which the words 'holy' and 'unholy' are contrived to appear.

A quarter of the population of Bangkok ('the City of Heavenly Being' – in Thai) lives in slums while in the wealthy section of the city the most luxurious high life is going on. Expensive automobiles of prestigious names are on the streets. Shop windows display the latest exclusive fashions from Europe. 'Bangkok is a good place', so say the exploiters. 'There is something obviously wrong with this city of heavenly beings' say the exploited. The city is sick. There is something *unholy* about this city.

Every year in September the New Zealand hills are spotted with millions of new born lambs. How beautiful and pastoral. In 1976, at this very time of nature's lovely creativity, there appeared, as it were from the abyss of darkness, two nuclear battleships visiting Wellington and Auckland, the iron mass capable of dealing immense destruction. Sheep on the rolling hills and the nuclear monsters. What a contrast. It would be too romantic to credit the sheep with holy attributes, perhaps, but there is something abominable about the multi-million-death-machines. Indeed, there is something *unholy* about the battleships.

The motorcycle has an engine. An engine produces technological (not spiritual!) power, fumes and noise. You may ride on it on Sri Ayutaya Road in Bangkok but you may not ride it into the courtyard of Wat Benjamabopit, the Marble Temple. The engine sound and the smell of fumes must stay outside the temple. One must not ride the motorcycle into the courtyard of mosques, churches and *wats*

(Thai Buddhist temples) because these are holy zones. There is incongruity between the technological and the spiritual. Mixing up of the two kinds of powers and two kinds of zones is an affront to the *holy*.

Japan is a land full of chimneys that spew black chemical smoke. Unless we smoke we will die. But if we smoke we will die too. Yet we must increase our GNP. What is the solution? Export our chimneys to South East Asian countries. To Mindanao. To West Malaysia. Do they welcome them? Yes. Those who will make money will allow importation of pollution. Exporters and importers have made a pollution conspiracy. I find this whole international situation chemically polluted. I find it *unholy*.

Sometime ago I was invited to watch an open heart operation at the Otago Medical School. A team of doctors and technicians moved around the quiet, apparently lifeless, patient as though they formed a living mandala at the centre of which is the ailing heart. Such dedication to save human life. I saw the set of sophisticated medical machines connected in a maze of lines and tubes. As I watched the operation I sensed an inspiring harmony of medical technology, science, skill and trained mental concentration. Here technology seemed to me to be something more than technology. I felt some mysticism of technology. I sensed there the presence of the *holy*.

Within a year of my first arrival in the United States as a student, I worked as an orderly in a State Psychiatric Hospital. In the surgical ward where I worked death was a frequent occurrence. One night I took care of a dying patient. In the dim light while all other patients were asleep I watched alone the last moments of this lonely American's life. I gave him his last water. I told myself; 'this is a *holy* moment because a person is dying'.

Why is there a touch of awkwardness attached to the use of the holy and the unholy in these paragraphs? The reason for this must be that the holy is a depth reality and not a surface-reality. It is present but it is hidden in depth. It is hidden but it is related and pervading. It comes to us in many forms in the context of our experience of life. It is there . . . in the depth.

> More than any other term, 'holiness' gives expression to the essential nature of the 'sacred'. It is therefore to be understood, not as one attribute among other attributes, but as the innermost reality to which all others are related. Even the sum of all the attributes and activities of 'the holy' is insufficient to exhaust its meaning, for to the one who has experienced its presence there is always a plus, a 'something more', which resists formulation or definition.[1]

This depth-holy, which is always 'something more', is focusing-holy. As it focuses itself around man it speaks the language of Deuteronomy; 'See I have set before you this day life and good, death and evil. . . . therefore choose life' (30.15–20). That which is unholy violates human dignity. Deep, pervading, focusing holy challenges us, confronting us with the choice of Deuteronomy. That 'medical technology points to the presence of the holy' means that human dignity has been upheld. There too 'the choice' must be constantly remembered. This is the holy-related-choice.

It is God who is holy. 'Holy, holy, holy is the Lord of hosts.' His glory – expression of his holiness – fills the whole earth.

8   At the Foundation of Our Life

In the beginning was the Word, and the Word was with God, and the Word was God.   *John 1.1*

'In the beginning' means 'at the foundation of'. At the foundation of all humanity and of all things was the Word. This *was* is a special 'theological' *was*. It means *is* and *will be* and *forever*! It is a living *was*. At the foundation of all *was, is, will be* and *forever* the Word of God. This is covenant language. We must take careful notice that it was the Word, neither noise nor sound which was in the beginning. '. . . and if the bugle gives an indistinct sound, who will get ready for battle' (I Cor. 13.8). William Temple says that actually John wanted to say that 'in the beginning was the Messiah'. But for the Greek audience which he was addressing he thought he would try to introduce the unfamiliar Hebraic Messiah, Jesus, by speaking about the familiar concept of the Word. 'In the beginning was the Word' means 'at the foundation of our life is the Person and Work of Jesus Christ'. Is this not a freeing and uniting thought?

The Word which was in the beginning comes to us as the Word of incarnation (Christmas), the Word of the cross (Good Friday) and the Word of resurrection (Easter). These Words are one Word. The incarnate Lord is the crucified Lord. The crucified Lord is the risen Lord. There is only one Jesus Christ, the Lord. No one can isolate incarnation from crucifixion, crucifixion from resurrection.

Crucifixion does not make sense apart from incarnation, the resurrection apart from crucifixion. Crucifixion is the ultimate depth of incarnation (Phil. 2. 6–8) and resurrection is the 'therefore' of crucifixion (v.9). We have no compartmentalized theology of incarnation, theology of cross and theology of resurrection. Theology is to do with the living continuous story of Jesus Christ and how in this life God revealed himself to us. 'He who has seen me has seen the Father' (John 14.9). Speaking like this does not mean that I am, as it were, in control of these great mysteries with regard to the life of Jesus Christ. None of us can stand above the inexhaustible meaning of incarnation, crucifixion and resurrection. '. . . for now we see in a mirror dimly' (I Cor. 13.12). What I do understand is that there is one Jesus Christ who was born, crucified and risen. And I believe that he is at the foundation of our life.

We learn of Jesus Christ through studying the Bible, in particular the New Testament. We do this as ones who belong to the community of faith. The story of Jesus Christ which we find in the New Testament gospels gives us the impression that the event of the cross of Christ illuminates, by the grace of God, the meaning of his life and death and resurrection. We feel that we can see the meaning of incarnation and resurrection more when we see them through the event of crucifixion. 'For I decided to know nothing among you except Jesus Christ and him crucified' declares the apostle Paul (I Cor. 2.2). I do not understand this powerful sentence to mean that he does not care about Christ's incarnation and resurrection. In the Christ crucified he must have found the most powerful summary of the whole ministry of Jesus Christ. 'But far be it from me to glory except in the cross of our Lord Jesus Christ, by which the world has been crucified to me, and I to the world' (Gal. 6.14).

The Word of the cross is the word of unfathomable self-denial. The hands of Jesus are nailed down. In such a painful defenceless form – compare the hands of crucified Jesus with those of Muhammad Ali who is ever defence-full – his self-denial is portrayed. Why in such a mutilated form?

Is his self-denial a sickly one? Isn't it true that often self-denial derives from a morbid mind? The apostolic witness says that his utter giving of himself is motivated by his love directed to man. The apostolic church has seen the glory of God in the crucified Jesus! (John 1.14) In this form God expressed his love to the world. 'For God so loved the world that he gave his only Son . . .' (John 3.16). How can we imagine that the Word which was in the beginning, the Word which is at the foundation of our life is such a living Word of utter self-denial for our sake! The one who denies himself frees and unites us. 'If any man would come after me, let him deny himself and take up his cross and follow me' (Matt. 16.24).

The Word of the cross is the word of reconciliation. Jesus Christ was rejected (Acts 4.5–12). Upon the cross he was rejected by God who remained silent. 'My God, my God, why hast thou forsaken me?' (Mark 15.34). Is such a thing possible? No one is ever so forsaken as Jesus Christ since no one is ever so close to God! The cry upon the cross came from the same man who said: 'I am not alone, for the Father is with me' (John 16.32). He was alienated from man and God. The apostle Paul writes to the Corinthians (II Cor. 6.16–21) that '. . . for our sake he made him to be sin who knew no sin, so that in him we might become the righteousness of God'. On this basis Paul beseeches us 'on behalf of Christ be reconciled to God'. The one who was most alienated, condemned and forsaken thus became the fountain head of reconciliation and so frees and unites humanity.

The Word of the cross is the word that communicates. There are a variety of communication-situations in our life. To receive a notice of a library fine for your overdue books is one kind of communication. To tell someone that Socrates was a Japanese is one kind of communication situation even though the contents of this communication contain a mistake. When I say the word of the cross is the word that communicates, I am thinking of things relating to that which is 'at the foundation of human life'. 'For the foolishness of God is wiser than men, and the weakness of God is stronger than men' (I Cor. 1.25) . . . the communication of God is wiser than that of men even though we do not immediately find so. The communication of God is stronger than that of men in the level of the foundation of our life. The one who is crucified is most communicating. God expresses his depth through the crucified Lord. God, in his mystery, decided to reveal his love to humanity in *this* form. 'For God so loved the world that he gave his only Son. . . .'

The power that enlivens communication is love. The great love is great communication, and *vice versa*. This is the secret of the enduring quality of the Christian faith. God is love. God is communicating. Both of these go together even though it is 'hidden' from us. Hidden yet most communicating communication. An unusual manner of communication, indeed.

9 Unity of Thinking Well and Purity of Heart

Blessed are the pure in heart, for they shall see God.

Matthew 5.8

Sometime ago I stood on the misty Wilmot Pass in New Zealand's Fjordland. I found myself in the silence of a primeval world. It was as though the silence had been unbroken for millions of years before I alighted from a tourist bus. As I walked away from the people, I could almost see dinosaurs lumbering in the valley below me. In that Fjordland primordial silence I felt myself so tiny, so insignificant and transient! The scholars say that our earth has existed for about four billion years. If this incredible duration of time were translated into the image of distance on the basis of one kilometer, then proportionately the duration of fifty years would occupy 0.0125 mm and 0.5 mm would represent the two thousand years of Christianity. This is a staggering thought. Silence and dinosaurs appeared to me to remind me of the cosmic perspective. I felt I was disappearing into the mists. I felt the primeval silence purified my soul. I think it did.

At that moment, I felt strongly; 'I am responsible to others,' I suddenly came to realize the need of my personality dancing with those of others. Is not this purification? 'Blessed are the pure in heart, for they shall see God'. What does 'pure in heart' mean if it is not the heart concerned about others? What does it mean if it is not the heart that motivates the personalities of all of us to dance together? Otherwise, 'pure in heart' will be an 'egoistic in heart'. An egoistic heart cannot be pure. How can that which diminishes the life of others be called pure? Can that which imprisons life be called blessed?

I saw dinosaurs only in my imagination – a healthy imagination, I hope. It started a more serious reflection. Silence overwhelmed me. Dinosaurs whispered to me. If our life-span is more or less around 0.0125 mm in the scale of one kilometer, does it not invite us to think about the relationship between quality and quantity?

> Man is but a reed, the most feeble thing in nature; but he is a thinking reed. The entire universe need not arm itself to crush him. A vapour, a drop of water suffices to kill him. But if the universe were to crush him, man would still be more noble than that which killed him, because he knows that he dies and the

advantage which the universe has over him; the universe knows nothing of this. All our dignity consists, then, in thought. By it we must elevate ourselves, and not by space and time which we cannot fill. Let us endeavour, then, to think well; this is the principle of morality.[2]

Four billion years is a long time. But the earth does not know it. We, who live only for fifty years, know it. This is our unique dignity. This is the secret and the glory of man. Our 'quantity' is drastically limited, but our 'quality' can elevate us to a great and noble height. Our ability to *think*. When we think we are different from all other creations. In thought man is man. In thought man is moral. When our morality is rooted in 'thinking well', our 0.0125 mm shines like a diamond. It outshines all other illuminations. 'The birth of thought' according to Teilhard de Chardin, distinguishes man from other living beings. Man is capable 'no longer merely to know, but to know oneself; no longer merely to know, but to know that one knows'[3].

I am grateful to the Creator for his gift of thinking. Yet, I cannot explain what is the difference between non-thinking and thinking. As soon as I think about non-thinking, I find myself thinking. I cannot explain where and how thinking comes from or how it functions. I know I think. I accept these inspiring passages of Pascal. I wish, however, to combine 'the dignity of man in thought' and 'the pure in heart'.

I believe that 'thinking well' and 'purity of heart' are intimately related. Hitler did not think-well in spite of all his '*Blitz Krieg* thinking'. He engaged in thinking in the direction of destruction. His way of thinking destroyed the foundation of morality. It was distorted, superficial and demonic. With single-mindedness he pursued the destruction of others and his own self-aggrandisement. Such 'purity' is impure. Such purity is immoral. Here the relationship between 'the dignity of man in thought' and 'the purity in heart' has been ruined.

Thinking-well is thinking well only when in it man sees God. So also, purity of heart is indeed purity of heart only when in it man sees God. Thinking-well and purity of heart meet in the point of 'seeing God'. Yet God remains unseen. It is not, then, an ordinary seeing. It is an extraordinary seeing. 'God' is the symbol for man's deepest sense of integrity. 'God' invites us to achieve in spirit the unity of thinking well and purity of heart.

In the article 'The United States and the Soviet Union, 1917–1976' George F. Kennan, who was once United States Ambassador to the Soviet Union, writes:

The recognition that the Russians had the weapon, and the necessary carriers, served as sufficient basis for the assumption that they had a desire to use it and would, if not deterred, do so. In part, this was the product of the actual discipline of peacetime military planning. The planner has to assume an adversary. In the case at hand, the Russians, being the strongest and the most rhetorically hostile, were the obvious candidates. The adversary must then be credited with the evilest of intentions. No need to ask *why* he should be moved to take certain hostile actions, or whether he would be likely to to take them. That he has the capability of taking them suffices. The mere fact that they would be damaging to one's own side is regarded as adequate motive for their execution. In this way not only is there created, for planning purposes, the image of the totally inhuman and totally malevolent adversary, but this image is reconjured daily, week after week, month after month, year after year, until it takes on every feature of flesh and blood and becomes the daily companion of those who cultivate it, so that any attempt on anyone's part to deny its reality appears as an act of treason or frivolity. Thus the planner's dummy of the Soviet political personality took the place of the real thing as the image on which a great deal of American policy, and of American military effort, came to be based.[4]

If Professor Kennan's view is correct, it means that this global grip of fear caused by the two superpowers is a result of 'not thinking well'. '. . . the planner's dummy of the Soviet political personality took the place of the real thing . . .' This situation does not represent a careful thinking. The superpowers have mutually created a totally malevolent image of each other. In support of that image both have engaged to build up an immense military arsenal. The cost of 'not-thinking-well' is astronomical. Some 200 billion dollars going to the production of military machines every year. This is immoral. The quality of 0.0125 mm of life is threatened. Our history is crippled. Our integrity is ruined.

Perhaps our failure in thinking well comes from our failure to live in purity of heart. Careless thinking and impurity of heart can make a dreadfully destructive combination. The brain must be guided by the heart. The heart must be enlightened by the brain. 'Seeing God' – that is, the realization of the most satisfying peace (*shalom*) – takes place among us when the dignity of man in his thinking well is combined with the grace of purity in heart.

10 'Where are You?' in Technological Age

Straightness is not natural. The human body is not made up of straight lines. The body of the fish impresses us with its mysteriously beautiful curves. The womb is not a cube. Straightness is not natural. It is technological. Technology is efficient. Straightness is efficient. The straight line is the shortest distance between two points. The shortest distance is an efficient distance. Straightness is artificial. It is man-made.

Nature is full of curves that embrace curves; acute curves and gentle curves. Curves produce irregular forms. Straightness contains only fragments of straight line. Human civilization is made up of nature and un-nature, un-artificial and artificial.

Straightness is a symbol of streamlined efficiency. Consider the Xerox copying machine. From the outside it looks like a small freezer into which you can store a side of calf. It is a shiny box with a few conveniently placed switches. From the outside it looks simple, problem-free, neat and orderly. But the inside of the Xerox machine is a completely different story. It is a confusing maze of lines of which I can understand nothing. But this complicated machine obeys me as I push a few simple buttons. I do not have to see the inside. I work only 'superficially' from the outside. It works for me. Technology is increasingly making us *outsiders*. It covers up all the confusing parts and presents to us only the attractive, simple side – shiny switches. We are prevented from seeing the process. We start the machine, then without doing anything we will have the result. The working part is *hidden*. Only the result is visible. This is what 'straightness' means.

Think of the super-express train in Japan. It runs from Tokyo to Osaka (515 kilometers) in 3 hours 10 minutes. We who are passengers do not see the parts of the train where the 'great work' is going on. We see only the attractive side. We ride on it in comfort. So it is also with the colour television set. It looks so simple from the outside. The smallest child can operate it. The whole world in its many aspects, beautiful and ugly, enters our living room on its screen. Yet we receive it without effort. Technological life makes us 'straight-minded'. It can *maya* us, if we use the Indian expression. *Maya* comes from *mā* meaning 'to frame'. Technology can surround us with an attractive efficient world. But it is a technologically framed world. *Maya* is often translated as 'illusion'.

How much technology can we use without being victimized by the technological *maya*? How much streamlining can we take and still be able to say that the meaning and structure of our human life has not been swallowed by technological efficiency? There is something deceptive about the 'streamlines'. It is a kind of plastic surgery. Can human life really be so neatly streamlined? A strange Burmese story comes to my mind:

> . . . . a young boy, who after being bitten by a cobra, was taken by his parents to a monk to be cured. The latter said that no medicine could cure the boy, but that he would attempt a cure by an act of truth. He said that in his fifty years in the robes he had been happy only during the first seven years following his ordination, and 'If I am telling the truth, let the poison flow out of this child's body.' When he uttered these words, the poison flowed from the boy's head to his chest. Then the father, saying he would tell a truth, said that he did not like to give *dana* (religious giving) although he had been doing it all his life. At this, the poison flowed from the boy's chest to his waist. Then the mother said she would tell a truth. She said that she had not been happy with her husband during their entire married life. At this, the poison flowed completely out of the boy's body.[5]

When crisis hits the family, attractive appearances do not help. The truth must come out. Unattractive, inefficient, un-streamlined human truth must be faced. The monk looks happy. The father is doing his religious obligation willingly. The mother is happily married. But there is a poison hidden under these social cosmetics. We want to present an acceptable front to others. Of course, who among us wants other people to see inside of us? Truth (*aletheia* in Greek) means 'non-concealment'. 'It thus indicates a matter or state to the extent that it is seen, indicated or expressed, and that in such seeing, indication or expression it is disclosed, or discloses itself, as it really is, with the implication, of course, that it might be concealed, falsified, truncated, or suppressed. *Aletheia*, therefore, denotes the "full or real state of affairs".'[6] Who among us wants to 'disclose' ourselves to others? We have secrets. We do not show all to the others. We let people see only portions, only the attractive parts.

> And they heard the sound of the Lord God walking in the garden in the cool of the day, and the man and his wife hid themselves from the presence of the Lord God among the trees of the garden. But the Lord God called to the man, and said to him, 'Where are you?'

We have a secret which we do not want God to know. But God is the one who comes persistently with the question 'Where are you?' And being thus asked we realize that we do not and cannot see the whole of ourselves. We are perhaps looking at ourselves 'technologically' – 'superficially' – 'efficiently'. When God comes with his question 'Where are you?' – we are placed in a crisis. Truth (non-concealment) will attack us. We are shown to ourselves. We experience then the movement of the poison. The question 'Where are you?' makes us 'insiders' about ourselves. Our relationship to ourselves will cease to be that of passengers on the super-express trains or viewers of the television set. We cannot remain 'quick-result-minded'. We cannot stay any longer behind our social cosmetics.

Recently I took a bus tour of Mexico City. A well-cushioned, comfortably airconditioned tourist bus took us around the most luxurious section of the city where we saw gorgeous houses and gardens. I have seen just such sections in Manila, Djakarta and Bangkok. The one in Manila is physically walled off from the other sections of the city. In Mexico City I made a special effort to see the large section of slums at the edge of the city. Only then I felt had I seen Mexico City. The train arriving in Bangkok Central Station from the northern districts goes through a slum section just before it arrives in the station. The beautiful green paddy fields suddenly give way to man-made filth, social injustice and mammoth human frustration just before you arrive at Central Station. This is an appropriate arrangement even though I don't think the government planned it to be so. Tourists must see this. Bangkok without the slum section is a half truth. It would be a 'streamlined' Bangkok. It is a Bangkok 'concealed, falsified, truncated and suppressed'. If I try to see the whole of Mexico City and whole of Bangkok, then, by the power of truth the poison of ignorance will flow out my head. . . . God's 'Where are you?' destroys our *maya* about ourselves.

I am not implying that we should reject technology. I welcome the washing machine, telephone, automobile and electric heater-blanket. The Xerox machine and the super-express train are useful to me. What I am saying is that a technologically comfortable life may *maya* us to see ourselves 'streamlined' and separate us from the truth (non-concealment) about ourselves. 'Where are you?' God discloses us to ourselves by this question. In our technological age God's 'Where are you?' comes to us again with fresh and urgent meaning.

11   Dying Jesus Creates Human Relationship

Those who were crucified with him also reviled him.   *Mark 15.32*

A dictionary says that *inhibition* is 'a mental or psychological process that restrains or suppresses an action, emotion or thought'. Inhibition has a positive value. Without inhibition how can I build a sound social relationship? A life-style without an element of inhibition must be chaotic. When I feel inhibited at least I know that I am thoughtful about how others would feel if I did this or that. But, . . . I wonder if the real reason for my inhibition is *fear* of rejection. I naturally seek acceptance by others. How am I to avoid possible rejection by others? How do I keep myself from burning? By not going near to the fire! Non-risking is an efficient method of self-protection. But, . . . is it not egoistic in the final analysis? Is it not a sterile and uninteresting personal protectionism? Is it not a porcupine life-style?

The porcupine life is an impoverished life because there is no place for others. When I avoid others, I am avoiding myself. When I reject others I am rejecting myself. When I find others, I find myself. When I restore others, I restore myself. Suppose I were lost in the woods, I would hope to find something or someone other than myself. I need to find the others to locate myself; a signpost? the tree I recognize? the location of the sun? There is no point in crying out; 'I see myself. As long as I see myself, I am not lost!' Precisely then I am lost. Strangely, 'I see myself' is a lost condition. I must see myself *among others*. Personality is not a static condition. Personality is an event. It takes place when there is meeting between myself and others. The porcupine personality is immobilized, imprisoned and fossilized. The over-inhibited personality is deprived of life-giving oxygen. If I feel my personality is suffocated, I must be suffering from over-inhibition, egoism, self-love. On the other hand, even though I feel inhibited, if my personality is not suffocating I must be under a sensible and useful inhibition.

Our personalities can actively move around in the space between you and me. Between us is the meaningful living space. It is better to eat half a plate of pizza in this living space than to eat the full plate alone. It is better to live and die in this space than to live outside of it. Outside we suffocate. In this space is life. In this space is time. In this space is fulfilment. Why? because it is in this space

that my personality can dance. It is in this space that I can be a
person, a fulfilling person.

Christ was crucified between the thieves. 'Those who were
crucified with him also reviled him.' This verse is important because
it indicates that Jesus Christ did not die alone. Even in this agonizing moment what the thieves did must be reported. They were
reviling Jesus. But in doing so, still they kept 'company' with Jesus.
They were remembered through the centuries with Jesus Christ.
They were introduced. They were introduced when Christ was
being crucified. The biblical God is the creator of relationship
among people. He introduces us at all cost. God respects man.
While we take the name of God in vain, he takes our names carefully. . . . what the thieves did was incorporated in the story of
salvation. The Bible says that God is love. Love is a far more
fundamental concept than that of inhibition. Love is willingness to
give oneself. Love must control inhibition. Inhibition subordinated
to love is creative.

12   Idolatrous Resourcefulness and Worshipful Resourcefulness

> The Lord called to him from the mountain and told him to say to the
> Israelites, Jacob's descendants: 'You saw what I, the Lord, did to the
> Egyptians and how I carried you as an eagle carries her young on her
> wings, and brought you here to me. Now, if you will obey me and keep my
> covenant, you will be my own people. The whole earth is mine, but you
> will be my chosen people, a people dedicated to me alone, and you will
> serve me as priests.'   *Exodus 19.3–6 (TEV)*

God carries us. Any 'god' we can carry is, according to Jeremiah,
an idol. 'Such idols are like scarecrows in a field of melons; they
cannot speak; they have to be carried because they cannot walk'
(10.5). That which we can carry is subject to our control. To suggest
that something that we can carry is carrying us is to have an up-
side-down perspective of life. Such a style of life would be confusing
and destructive. Idolatry is just such a confusion. Carrying scarecrows, we do not insult them nor hurt ourselves. It is not up-side-
down. But in trying to carry the living God of Mount Sinai, the

God of Abraham, Isaac and Jacob, we insult him and we destroy ourselves. In doing so we will eventually be overcome by fear.

Fear is not unrelated to confusion. If one sees a piece of rope in the darkness and takes it to be a snake, he will certainly be frightened by the confusion. If we know rope to be rope and snake to be snake, we will be free from unnecessary fear. When man is elevated to god, or something more than man, fear stalks into history. 'Mussolini is always right' proclaimed the Fascist Decalogue of 1938. 'We, by the grace of Heaven, Emperor of Japan, seated on the throne of a line unbroken for ages eternal, enjoin upon you, our loyal and brave subjects; . . . .' began the opening sentence of the Imperial Rescript of 8 December 1941 declaring war on the United States and Great Britain. Strangely and tragically idolatrous confusion can attract immense human devotion. Even reputable philosophers began to substantiate the ultra rightist idolatrous nationalism during the war.

'I carried you as an eagle carries her young on her wings.' This is the fundamental character of the reign of God. The reign of God begins with God's initiative. God carries us. We do not carry God. No matter how resourceful we are, we are not to 'carry God'. Genuine resourcefulness comes from the experience of 'being carried by God' instead of 'carrying God'. This, however, is against our liking. We still want to identify resourcefulness with 'carrying God'. 'If any man would come after me, let him deny himself and take up his cross and follow me' says Jesus (Matt. 16.24). We are so 'resourceful'. We do not want to follow him. Jesus is too slow! We want to run before him. In evangelism? Yes. The way of Jesus is too slow, inefficient and painful. Jesus' resourcefulness is love. Ours is money. We adjust Matthew 16.24 to the high-powered methodology of Madison Avenue. We feel obliged to carry Jesus. He is not as resourceful as we would like. He is not as spectacular as we had hoped. He is not as exciting as we expected. We have to carry him!

. . .

But biblical resourcefulness comes from the experience of 'being carried by God'.

The human endeavour to carry the God of Abraham, Isaac and Jacob distorts the basic perspective of salvation. In our idolatrous resourcefulness we give a 'job description' to God and define his 'terms of service' for us. God is changed into a god of fertility cult. His job – for which he receives his salary – is to keep us prosperous. He is a high class hired servant to guarantee our happiness. The image of the 'eagles' wings' stands against such idolatrous resourcefulness. We are carried by God and become resourceful. This is a worshipful resourcefulness.

Salvation invokes discipline. No easy or lazy life will follow salvation. Salvation is the beginning and foundation of our responsible life. So, also, is the prologue to the Ten Commandments in the next chapter; 'I am the Lord your God who brought you out of the land of Egypt, out of the house of bondage. You shall have no other gods before me . . .' (Exod. 20.2f.). Affirmation of salvation comes first, then the Ten Commandments. This is the biblical order. So the *if* in our passage is carefully placed. 'Now *if* you will obey me and keep my covenant, you will be my own people.' You *are* my people *and* you *will be* my people. You are my people because of what I did to you. You will be my people if you keep my covenant. The second can come because of the first. The first is the context in which the second is spoken.

Will you obey me and keep my covenant? What a direct question! I have brought you to *me*. So may I address you personally and directly? Do you appreciate what I have done? That appreciation will become the sign of your being my people. That appreciation, that is your *response* to what I have done, will make you 'my chosen people'. That appreciation will make you priests, the people with the sign of the reign of God. You will be the sign to 'the whole earth' which is mine. You shall be no longer hemmed in a narrow space of fear. You are taken out of the narrow space into the 'whole earth' of freedom. Anyone who lives with the appreciation of the eagle's wings and *therefore* wishes to live for others is a priest in the whole earth which is God's. The reign of God becomes a reality in our world through this response.

To be priest does not mean to be able to manoeuvre or manipulate God. It means to be appreciative of what God has done for man's salvation. God carries us. Appreciation for this is the secret of our priestly energy and active life.

13 Technology and Wrinkled Faces and Rough Hands

More than that, we rejoice in our sufferings, knowing that suffering produces endurance, and endurance produces character, and character produces hope, and hope does not disappoint us, because God's love has been poured into our hearts through the Holy Spirit which has been given to us.

Romans 5.3–5

Air New Zealand has a fleet of sleek modern jet planes staffed by beautiful air hostesses. I have just returned from Moscow, having attended a church meeting there. To compare the old Russian women whom I saw in the churches there with the hostesses on the New Zealand planes may seem an odd thing to do. But allow me this liberty because the comparison has spoken something to me. It looks something like this:

wrinkled, careworn face	smooth, shining face
wearing thick heavy boots	wearing slender high heels
no make-up	cosmetics used to best advantage
no hair-do	sophisticated hair style
carrying all kinds of burdens	carrying only stylish hand-bag and light luggage
appearing weary and tired	always fresh and attractive
smelling of earth and sweat	smelling of expensive perfume

I would prefer to have dinner with someone from the second column rather than from the first. The hostesses are beautiful. Their beauty is obvious. They are attractive. Their attractiveness is direct. It is there. It is straightforward.

Watching the Russian women I saw Romans 5.3–5. In their wrinkled faces and rough hands I saw trouble that produced endurance. How hard they must have worked all through their lives with those hands. I thought of the hands of the Buddhist image, Bodhisattva, too beautiful as compared with these hands of the Russian women. Merciful hands must show themselves as hard, worn hands, not as beautiful, attractive hands. How eloquent are those rough, tired hands. They speak of severe Russian winters, of cooking meals and washing clothes, floors, cooking pots in poorly heated houses. They fended off despair by working, working on through intolerable situations. Endurance brings God's approval. In endurance life is taken seriously. Trouble is not cheated or avoided. It is faced. Honest endurance brings God's approval. He who avoids trouble or hardship by cheating and exploiting others is not facing the reality of life. He cheats himself. By cheating himself, he cheats God. But through endurance, to feel that life is surrounded by the warm approval of God, will that not be the experience of hope? Hope is in spite of troubles. There is no hope apart from troubles. There is no automatic hope, no easy hope. Hope is hope against all odds. Such hope, says Paul, does not end in disappointment.

Hope which is not backed by love is a false hope. Love produces wrinkles and rough hands. Love substantiates hope. Rough hands substantiate hope. Hope points to the presence of the Holy Spirit in this world. The Holy Spirit has something to do, then, with the wrinkled faces and rough hands. The Holy Spirit is the Spirit of Jesus Christ. In his hands are the scars of crucifixion.

The old Russian women are 'theologically' beautiful. They make me think. They bring me to repentance. They show me the presence of the Holy Spirit in the world. The beauty of the New Zealand air hostesses is direct and immediate. The beauty of the Russian women is hidden. It is to be found only after much living. Why, then, do middle aged wealthy women from Singapore, Manila and Bangkok fly to Japan to undergo expensive plastic surgery to take away the lines of life from their faces?

Advanced technology is with us today. Only eight hours from Singapore to Tokyo. There another technology is waiting for you to eradicate the wrinkles from your face. Washing machines will do washing for us. Water is always comfortably warmed for our use. Just by switching on, we will have our room immediately warmed. Rain cannot bother us because our car will protect us from getting wet by the rain. Our life today is surrounded by a system of remote controls. Our hands and our fingers are preserved in good condition since machines do work for us. Technology is then making all of us more or less look like the New Zealand air hostesses. It is eradicating the traditional symbol of 'wrinkled faces and rough hands' from our life. The more remote controls we have, the more soft and beautiful will be our hands.

What is there to replace the great tradition of the 'wrinkled faces and rough hands'? That which is symbolized by the 'wrinkled faces and rough hands' is essential for human life if it is to remain meaningful.

14   Turban Ablaze

I know your works; you are neither cold nor hot. Would that you were cold or hot! So, because you are lukewarm, and neither cold nor hot, I will spew you out of my mouth.   *Revelation 3.15,16*

There is a short simile of the Buddha which neatly summarizes the fundamental message of Buddhism. It is called 'Turban Ablaze'.

Monks, when one's turban or head is ablaze, what is to be done?
Lord, when one's turban or head is ablaze, for the extinguishing
thereof one must put forth extra desire, effort, endeavour, exertion, impulse, mindfulness and attention.

The Buddha agrees with the response given by his monks. It
requires an all-out battle to extinguish this fire. It is an extremely
difficult fire to combat. For all of our turbans are ablaze with
ignorance and greed. The situation is of great urgency. Not our
trousers but our turbans, our heads, are ablaze. This, according to
the Buddha, is the truth about man. We may call it 'religious truth',
but it is plainly human truth. It is not revelation. It is rooted in a
critical analysis of man. Analyse yourself! Study yourself! You will
know it by yourself! Our turbans are ablaze!

I may very well answer the Buddha that my turban is not ablaze.
I may, thus, avoid a sense of urgency. If my turban is indeed not
ablaze I need have no concern. But suppose it is in truth ablaze
and I protest that it is not, then I am in a fatal predicament. The
Buddha saw this to be true of man. Those who say 'my turban is
not ablaze', will be at leisure. They will not have a sense of urgency.
They will experience the truth about man differently from that
suggested by the Buddha.

'Those who are well have no need of a physician, but those who
are sick; I came not to call the righteous, but sinners' (Mark 2.17).
If you think you are well, you will naturally not seek a physician.
You stand at a distance from the physician. You live in a state of
non-urgency.

Non-urgency characterizes the life-style that is 'neither cold nor
hot'. Urgency comes when we realize that we are sick, or in the
simile of the Buddha, when we realize that our turban is ablaze.
The Buddha suggests that we 'must put forth extra desire, effort,
endeavour, exertion, impulse, mindfulness and attention' to extinguish it. Christ says, 'I came not to call the righteous, but sinners'.
It seems to me that both Buddha and Christ cannot really help
those who are 'neither cold nor hot'.

15   Bridge and Cross

And he said to them, 'My soul is very sorrowful, even to death; remain here, and watch.'
Mark 14.34

For five months I lived outside of San Francisco. The graceful and majestic Golden Gate Bridge became a part of my life. The bridge spans a distance of 6,450 feet to connect northern California to the peninsula of San Francisco. The bridge has six lanes for traffic. It's width is 90 feet. In the morning and evening the bridge is filled with automobiles travelling at the speed of fifty and sixty miles an hour.

In sixteen steps I walk over a small bridge in the Dunedin Botanical Garden. Sometimes I see ducks under the bridge. A small and quiet bridge all to myself. But this, too, is a bridge. Three billy goats cross a bridge. The secret of the fascination of this children's story must be the element of bridge that connects this side with that side. The bridge is a thought provoking arrangement, whether we go *tip tap tip tap* over it or in a car at fifty miles an hour.

A bridge is usually over a stream or river. A river has spirits. The spirits must be kept happy. They were happy in the time when there were no bridges. Swimmers drowned, boats capsized – and so the spirits were properly 'fed' from time to time. But the making of the bridges changed the situation. So the spirits dislike bridges. They consider them an insult. In ancient Rome, every year on 15 May a ceremony of sacrifice was performed on the oldest bridge (Saburica) over the Tiber. Twenty-four straw dolls made into the image of old people were violently thrown into the river to appease the spirits. As I cross over a bridge I can understand the feeling behind this ceremony. Upon the bridge is safety and under the bridge is massive raging water menacingly whirling and running. The water threatens. It wants to get you. The bridge has the powerful symbolism of crossing from this side to the other side over danger.

Tip tap tip tap . . . one by one the three goats cross the bridge. Crossing the bridge is inevitably an exciting moment, because it is accompanied by the sneaking sense of danger. Your familiar land is not beneath you. What is under you is danger. It is a psychologically heightened moment. Why do these three goats cross the bridge? It appears to them that the grass on the other side is greener. So they are migrating from this side (less prosperity) to that side (more prosperity). The bridge is a possibility of this movement between two worlds. Millions of people migrated from Europe to America. Three billy goats perform a symbolic act for us. The monster under the bridge is a disgruntled creature. It says 'I am going to eat you up!' All bridges threaten the users of the bridge, the migrants. So negotiation will ensue. The three billy goats engage in negotiation. They make a workable arrangement in the face of serious difficulty. The first two goats speak a strange language, a mixture of selfishness and community-mindedness. The biggest one is coming after us and he is responsible for our community. Would you settle the issue of migration with him. And . . . you know, . . . he will provide you with a bigger meal than we! Strange negotiation! They did not say; 'If you attack us, my big brother will come and beat you up!' Through this strange negotiation the two cross the threatening bridge to the other side. The third one comes. Here negotiation becomes confrontation. He confronts the monster and successfully beats him up. Victoriously he crosses the bridge, *clop, clop, thrump, thrump.* . . . This short story has all the excitement of life; the other side looking better, nervously crossing the bridge, encountering with danger, skillful negotiation, head-on collision between the powers, and victory. The centre of all this is the symbol of the bridge.

The bridge relates two separate zones. If those zones are this world and that world, the here and the beyond, then it is a strongly religious symbolism. Religion reveals its inner dynamic when it inspires people to move from *here* to *beyond*, self to selflessness, hate to love, chaos to cosmos, damnation to salvation. The most important priesthood in ancient Rome was the *collegium* of *pontifices* (builders and guardians of bridges). The word *pontifex* (*pons*, bridge, *facere*, to make) means bridgemaker. From here is the word *Pontifex Maximus* meaning both the Roman Emperor and the Pope of the Church of Rome. Pontiff then is the 'bridgebuilder'. Here the language of the bridge symbolism has been incorporated into the life of the church. Zoroaster says that each soul must face judgment at the Bridge of the Separator. The righteous soul will be accompanied by Zoroaster. The evil soul will fall down to the 'House of the Lie' (Hell) by its own guilt consciousness. A self-propelled fall. In the Jodo Buddhism (Pure Land Buddhism) of Japan the *Amida* Buddha will come at the moment of his devotee's death and take the soul to the world beyond, the bliss of Pure land. There is something deeply religious about the bridge symbolism.

Strangely, however, the New Testament does not impress us with the symbolism of the bridge. Jesus Christ is not a bridge from this world to that world upon which we safely walk over the danger.

The central symbolism of the Christian faith, the cross, does not give us an image of bridge. It gives us, instead, the feeling of confrontation, encounter and conflict. It is the point at which people meet. It is an image of intersection. The main emphasis here is not of a safe passage from damnation to salvation or of connecting this world with that world or of bringing the heaven principle (male) together with the earth principle (female). The cross stands for encounter and conflict and painful solution. It points to the place where we must stop. Why stop? Because it is there that *love* is expressed.

'My soul is very sorrowful, even to death; remain here, and watch.' Jesus Christ does not walk over the sorrow on a bridge. He stays on in the tribulation and by staying there he reveals his love to us. The bridge brings a happy ending. Without the 'bridge' then, Christianity is not a happy ending religion. It does not allow us to walk easily from this side to that side. It asks us to 'remain here and watch' and deepen our practice and understanding of love. There is a difference between the symbolism of bridge and that of the cross.

The Golden Gate Bridge is graceful and efficient. The small bridge in the botanical garden is very charming. I appreciate the bridge. I appreciate its efficiency and safety. Yet, every time I cross the bridge I compare these two images and remember the word of Jesus, 'remain here and watch'.

II World Meeting

16 Promised Land – Its Geography and Theology

> Now the Lord said to Abram, 'Go from your country and your kindred and your father's house to the land that I will show you.'   *Genesis 12.1*

The geography of the biblical promised land interests me. It is the land that God promised to give to Abraham and his descendants. 'The land that I will show you' was not Hawaii, the land of juicy pineapples, tall coconut trees, clear blue water, bright life-giving sunshine and abundant rainfall. It was a tiny corridor land placed right at the point where three continents meet: Asia, Africa and Europe. It was a busy, dangerous, unsettling intersection-land. On one side it is washed by the water of the Great Sea where the monsters dwell. It was this intersection-land that was the promised land to be given to the promised people. Abraham was called 'from Ur of the Chaldeans to go into the land of Canaan' (Gen. 11.31). Abraham, Isaac and Jacob were all hit by severe famine in the promised land and had to seek help from Egypt. The history of the people of Israel is, to use a Thai figure of speech, like living between a crocodile (Egyptian empire) and a tiger (the Assyrian and Babylonian empire). Briefly, this is an amazing geography for the biblical promised land.

Promised life then means intersected life. It is not an isolated life. It is a life busily engaged in encounters. It is a life not at home on the museum shelf. It is on-the-street-life. Christian faith is the heir to this promised-land-life. It hears the Word of God at intersections since the Lord of the church, Jesus Christ, lived a promised-land-life, an intersected life, and was crucified upon the intersected cross. He, the Promised One is, as it were, Mr Intersection.

Jesus spoke the dialect called Galilean Aramaic and the New Testament was written in the *koine* Greek. There was already a profound process of interpretation and accommodation going on in the very literature of the New Testament itself. The New Testament was not written in the confines of Galilean Aramaic but in many places within the then great Roman Empire. The New Testament itself, then, carries the character of intersected-life. In this sense it is the promised land literature. It is an encounter literature. Young Christianity was challenged when she came into the powerful context of Hellenistic and Egyptian religious cultures. This 'Mediterranean Encounter' enriched Christian life and helped to clarify the fundamental nature of the gospel of Jesus Christ. Yet it was a time of genuine crisis, the description of which is beyond the scope of this present discussion.

What I am bringing home is that perhaps the second critical encounter in the life of Christianity is now going on. It is her encounter with the Asian world, the world of great spiritual and religious heritages. I must be careful here lest I give you the impression that it is only in the last hundred years or so that Christianity came to Asia. Francis Xavier, church history's towering evangelist, landed in Kagoshima, Japan in 1549 and stayed in Japan for twenty-seven months. The first mass in the Philippines was said on Sunday, 31 March 1521. In 1546 even before his visit to Japan, Francis Xavier had laboured nine months in the Indonesian Moluccas. In the year 1601 Matthew Ricci entered Peking and in 1605 Robert De Nobili arrived in India and remained in South India for fifty years. We also know that Nestorian influence reached China during the early T'ang Dynasty (618–907). And in south-west India the very ancient church of the 'Thomas Christisna' still exists, claiming to be the fruit of the labour of St Thomas himself. Christianity has made significant inroads to Asian life particularly since the sixteenth century. The twentieth-century Philippines cannot be understood in any way apart from the understanding of her three hundred and fifty years under Spanish Catholicism.

This second encounter though in one sense going on for centuries, is now intensified and universalized. It is intensified and universalized because the world has shrunk. The theological meaning of the shrunken world is that the whole world is taking the shape of the geography of the promised land. Wherever you are today, you cannot but be 'encounter people' and 'intersection people'. We are all now promised land people. The geography of the promised land and the psychology of intensified human relationship go together. The peoples of different living faiths and ideology are encountering each other and living together. It is no longer 'elite-encounter'. It is becoming massive.

Our world has progressively become an assimilation world. Soon perhaps we may see as many Greek, Italian and other foreign shop signs as English ones in parts of Melbourne. Zurich, a classic Reformation city, now has a mosque for the university students from Islamic countries. In spite of all sorts of serious problems caused by this massive global reorganization, I think this process of transition from the world of many tribes to the world of one humanity is a blessing of God. How are we to make this process a creative, reconciling and educational one? This is the question posed to us by our shrinking world.

Today we are all standing at intersections. This means that we are all inter-dependent. Asia must learn theology from the West and West must learn theology from Asia in order to make the life of the world church rich, enlightened and more obedient to the mind of Jesus Christ, the Promised One who died on the cross.

17   Adam Awakened and Adam Asleep

God called the light Day, and the darkness he called Night. And there was evening and there was morning, one day.   *Genesis 1.5*

We are all involved in the subjects of cosmos and chaos. We live daily in a cosmos threatened by chaos, or perhaps chaos is threatened by cosmos! We cannot understand the value of one without the other. Man is a cosmological being. In Japanese the word for 'man' is said and written in two ways; *hito* (person) and *nin-gen* (*nin*, person, *gen*, 'in between'). Actually *nin-gen* means 'person' only in the secondary sense. Primarily it means 'where man lives' which comes close to the Greek word cosmos. The Chinese tradition has taught the Japanese people that the concept of man stands in an intimate association with the concept of cosmos, and therefore chaos. That cosmos is an orderly universe and the orderly universe is salvation is an eminently Greek idea. Disorder disrupts well-being and salvation. Whatever is aesthetically attractive is salvationally attractive.

Man named the animals (Gen.. 2.19f.). God named too! He did so before man began to do so. God named something quite basic. Day, Night, Heaven, Earth, and Sea (vv. 6–13). Why can't Adam name *all* things including Day, Night, Heaven, Earth and Sea? Why is there this limitation on Adam?

In every naming act man must remember that God preceded him. Adam names the woman. 'This at last is bone of my bones and flesh of my flesh; she shall be called Woman, because she was taken out of Man' (Gen. 2.23). The woman was prepared while he was in a deep sleep. This sleep was caused by God, 'theological sleep'. It was a strange unprecedented deep sleep during which the Creator worked.

There are two major living thoughts current in our world today. One looks at the universe remembering that Adam was asleep at one critical moment in the time of creation. It signifies that Adam cannot establish his own self-identity and his place in the cosmos unless he makes important reference to the one who put him into a 'deep sleep'. The knowledge of the deep sleep makes understanding of the cosmos salvational and meaningful. This tradition maintains an attitude of theological enchantment with the cosmos. Isn't it an enchanting thought that all things are created and sustained by the loving Creator . . . while man is 'in a deep sleep'?

The other looks at the universe as though Adam had not had such a 'transcendental sleep'. In truth he was awake. He is therefore the centre of all things and *he* named all things. If Adam did sleep it is caused by himself, not by 'God'. May I call the first thought 'self-identity with the deep sleep' and the other 'self-identity without the deep sleep'.

Asia has been historically enriched by two great living traditions; (1) India-China tradition, and (2) the Judaeo-Christian-Islamic tradition.

India invites us to spiritual enlightenment by way of spiritual discipline and maturity. Here *spiritual wisdom* is the central value. China speaks the philosophy of maintenance and change of the order in our political and cosmological life. It emphasizes the importance of *practical wisdom*. Thus, both India and China are *Wisdom* oriented, one in a spiritual and the other a more practical way. Chaos is the result of ignorance in either case.

In contrast to the wisdom emphasis of India and China, the Judaeo-Christian-Islamic tradition has given us the sense of *having God as Thou* (Encounter). When God (not gods) is introduced, sometimes even as 'jealous God', the sense of encounter is strengthened. Man's responsible individuality is discovered in the light of this Thou-God. There has now been influence strong enough in this tradition to change the historical awareness of the Asian peoples.

Asia is thus blessed with two types of truth; *Wisdom* and *Encounter*. The former tends to be 'self-identity without the deep sleep' (wisdom is possessed by the Awakened One, *Buddha*) and the latter strongly adheres to 'self-identity with the deep sleep'. (My help comes from the Lord, who made heaven and earth. . . . Behold, he who keeps Israel will neither slumber nor sleep' Psalm 121.2,4.) Over many centuries, then, we Asians have lived in the context of a historic dialogue between 'Adam awakened' and 'Adam asleep'. We are supposed to have a great deal of experience in this.

God named Day, Night, Heaven, Earth, and Sea. The most basic cosmological orders are named by God. Man did not name all things. How shall we appreciate this within our own Asian context of *wisdom* and *encounter?*

18   Impartiality of God

There will be tribulation and distress for every human being who does evil, the Jew first and also the Greek, but glory and honour and peace for everyone who does good, the Jew first and also the Greek. For God shows no partiality.   *Romans 2.9–11*

What the apostle Paul said here to the congregations in metropolitan Rome, where a great variety of races and religious experiences were living together, is of great importance for our understanding of the gospel of Christ today. He is not laying down a philosophical ethical principle. He is saying that the God of Israel, the God, the Father of Jesus Christ, shows no partiality. It is an apostolic confession. The Jew means the chosen people, the people of the covenant. 'We are descendants of Abraham. . . .' (John 8.33). They had experienced the salvation drama of exodus, exile and restoration. The law was given to them. Prophets came out of them. Finally Jesus Christ, himself a Jew, came from among this people. Indeed they are a quite special people. They are 'theological' people. Yet, Paul says that 'there will be tribulation and distress for every human being who does evil, the Jew first and also the Greek. . . . God shows no partiality'. The Jew comes first. Don't we hear the echo of the prophet Amos: 'O people of Israel, against the whole family which I brought up out of the land of Egypt; "you only have I known of all the families of the earth; therefore I will punish you for all your iniquities" ' (3.1,2).

Romans 2.9–11 has been unpopular in the history of Christian missions. Missionaries came to Asia and preached Romans 3.21,22: 'But now the righteousness of God has been manifested apart from law, although the law and the prophets bear witness to it, the righteousness of God through faith in Jesus Christ for all who believe.' They were right! This is the gospel. But certainly this proclamation of the gospel does not mean the abolishment of the impartiality of God. Are we who live in the grace of God in Jesus Christ free from the thought that 'God is not partial'? Is 2.9–11 only a preparatory step towards the gospel? Is it only, as it were, an appetizer to the main course? Or is it a part of the gospel?

What I have found out is this: 3.21,22 loses its theological punch whenever 2.9–11 is ignored. 3.21,22 divorced from 2.9–11 brings forth only a cheap gospel and a superficial discipleship. The cheap gospel is a distortion of the gospel. Superficial discipleship does damage to the work of the household of God. True, our message is about 'the righteousness of God through faith in Jesus Christ for all who believe'. But it must be said together with the awesome message of the impartiality of God, since this message belongs to the central part of the gospel of Christ. It is Good News to know that God is not partial. It would be Bad News to know that God is partial.

God speaks to us impartially as we live in this shrunken world today. Mankind are all neighbours to each other. We are in close contact with each other whether we like it or not. Even with a genius in Downing Street, Britain cannot solve its problems internally. China seeks United States technical help to modernize herself. Political upheaval in Iran has global repercussions. There are no longer such things as 'internal problems'. We are living within an increasingly close network of human frustration, aspiration and spirituality. God speaks an impartial word to this small world. In this historic juncture of mankind's life, the message that 'God is not partial' has become very important. For it is here that Christianity finds the basis to remain and develop as a universal faith for mankind today.

Asia can readily accept what Paul said to the Roman congregations. 'There will be tribulation and distress for every human being who does evil, the Christians first and also the Buddhists, Moslems, Animists. For God shows no partiality.' On this basis we must build our theology in our shrunken world. Asian Christians and perhaps even more the Asians who are not Christians are sensitive to the Christian message of the impartiality of God. They are challenging the church to hold fast to this message and examine itself. Has the church not lived in self-confidence and self-admiration forgetting that God, the Father of Jesus Christ, is not partial. Has not the church been parochial in its understanding of peoples of other living faiths and ideologies? Jesus Christ frees and unites. We must dare say that he does so impartially. Does not this mean judgment to us? Is not our stable theological system shaken? God's promise shakes us. Such theology free from tribalism and parochialism will demonstrate Jesus Christ powerfully today.

19   Christianity Suffers from 'Teacher Complex'

> Go therefore and make disciples of all nations, baptizing them in the name of the Father and of the Son of the Holy Spirit, teaching them to observe all that I have commanded you.   *Matthew 28.19–20*

The theme of this meditation is evangelism. I begin, however, by confessing that to all appearances the future of Christianity is in jeopardy. My reason for saying this is rather simple. It is because Christianity has become so self-righteous that I do not see much future for it. It wants to teach. It does not want to learn. It is arrogant. It is suffering from a 'teacher complex'. 'God, I thank thee that I am not like other men, extortioners, unjust, adulterers, or even like this tax collector. . . .' There is not much future in this type of religion.

Christianity is a religion. You may protest against this. 'All right', you say, 'if Christianity is a religion, it is a genuine and true religion over against other misguided, false and man-made religions. Christianity is a faith in the living God in Christ and therefore not a religion in an ordinary sense!'

Let us remember that Christianity is not identical with Jesus Christ. A Christian is not Jesus Christ. Christians are supposed to be 'Christ-like' but they are only rarely so. Whether we are discouraged at this or not, it is a fact. There is distance between Jesus Christ and Christianity as we know it. 'Not everyone who says to me "Lord, Lord" shall enter into the Kingdom of heaven, but he who does the will of my Father who is in heaven' (Matt. 7.21). The religion in which Jesus Christ is called 'Lord, Lord' is Christianity. But it is very possible that Christians, who call Jesus Christ, 'Lord,

Lord' do not do 'the will of my Father'. This observation should not shock us. In Paul's letter to the Corinthians, which was written about AD 53 or 54, the apostle spoke about divisions within the church (I Cor. 1.10–17). Division within the church is not 'the will of my father'. If we think everything was fine in the primitive church but later degenerated, we are mistaken.

Christianity is a historically developed religion just as Hinduism, Buddhism and Islam are. There is, then, no such thing as a divine, pure and uncontaminated Christianity. As a religion, Karl Barth says, Christianity with other religions must stand under the judgment of the gospel of Christ. 'There will be tribulation and distress for every human being who does evil, the Jew first and also the Greek, but glory and honour and peace for everyone who does good, the Jew first and also the Greek. For God shows no partiality'. (Rom. 2.9–11).

This religion called Christianity is, it seems to me, most interested in teaching people, but not interested in being taught by people. It speaks to people, but it does not listen to them. I do not think Christianity in Asia for the last 400 years has really listened to the people. It has ignored people. Ignoring *things* is not so bad, but ignoring *people* is serious. It has listened to its bishops, theologians and financial sponsors. But it really has not listened to the people. It might have listened to God (?) but it did not listen to its neighbours. 'Give me a drink' – Jesus sought help from a Samaritan woman (John 4.7) 'What is your name?' – Jesus asked a madman (Mark 5.9). In the famous story of evangelism of the chief tax collector, Zacchaeus, Jesus said only 'Zacchaeus, make haste and come down; for I must stay at your house today' (Luke 19.5). He was observing. He was listening. In the gospels, don't we get a strong impression that Jesus was not a talkative man, but that he was a careful listener?

Christianity has been busy planning mission strategy – this campaign and that crusade. People have become the object of evangelism since it is understood by Christians that people are 'automatically' living in the darkness, untrustworthy, wicked, adulterous and unsaved, while the believers are 'automatically' living in the light, trustworthy, good, not lustful, and saved. The 'teacher complex' expresses itself in a 'crusade complex'. What a comfortable arrangement for the believers! What an irresponsible and easygoing theology!

Christianity has become a one-way-traffic-religion. It is true that Christianity has done much to benefit mankind but it would have done much more if it had not suffered from this teacher complex. Let's be critical about ourselves. The Christian faith demands such self-criticism. Often this one-way set-up has been justified by simply quoting the Great Commission of the Risen Lord: 'Go therefore and make disciples of all nations, baptizing them in the name of the Father and of the Son and of the Holy Spirit, teaching them to observe all that I have commanded you' (Matt. 28.19–20). I do not understand this powerful sentence as an authorization for 'one-way-traffic'. I believe it calls for 'Christ-like going'. Take note that it says not just 'go' but 'go therefore', that is to say, go on the basis of the life and ministry of Jesus Christ, his love, his self-denial, his hope, his death, his resurrection. Only so are we to make disciples of all nations. 'Christ-like going' is not 'one-way-traffic'. It is intensely two-ways. And in this two-way-traffic situation with his people, he gave up his right of way! 'The Son of man came not to be served but to serve, and to give his life as a ransom for many' (Matt. 20.28). At the last moment of his life he was mocked by the 'church leaders'. 'So also the chief priests, with the scribes and elders, mocked him, saying "He saved others; he cannot save himself. He is the King of Israel; let him come down now from the cross, and we will believe in him" ' (Matt. 27.41–42).

We must read Matthew 28.19,20 together with Matthew 27.41–44 or with 16.24,25 – where Jesus tells his disciples, 'If any man would come after me, let him deny himself and take up his cross and follow me. For whoever would save his life will lose it, and whoever would lose his life for my sake will find it.' If we go we must be prepared to go the way of self-denial. We want to go, but we do not want to be mocked. Bishops, theologians and church leaders are prepared to go as long as their spiritual, intellectual and ecclesiast-ical prestige is safely protected. Do we mean – do we really mean – what we sing? 'Faith of our fathers, holy faith, we will be true till death'? Let's not sing what we do not mean. Lie begets lie. Soon we will hypnotize ourselves into believing lie is truth.

The amazing thing – how utterly amazing – is that it is only in this way of giving up himself that Christ came to us. In his self-denial he came to us. In his dying for us he came to us. This is the heart of the gospel. With the realization of this truth the apostolic faith began. Meditation on the crucified Lord – this is the theme of Christian spirituality and Christian mission.

One-way-traffic Christianity is an ugly monster. This monster lives by self-assertion, not by self-denial. Ugly? Yes. One-way-traffic human relationship is ugly. I understand that 'to be human' means to live in two-way traffic and 'to be divine' means to give up one's right-of-way for the sake of the other in this two-way traffic. The crusade concept is a product of Christianity, not of Christ. The word is not in the Bible. It raises its head like a cobra in modern

Christianity.

My occasional crusades against my wife, children and friends have always ended in unhappiness and alienation. I learned that by crusading I cannot run my own family. I don't think then that crusading has a place in the household of God. 'Crusade' is a self-righteous pharisaic (holy war) military word. It does not belong to the language of the 'Prince of Peace who died on the Cross'. I am hesitant to sing 'Stand up, stand up. . . .' because the hymn does not express the centre of the biblical message that 'in dying he came to us'. It is therefore too cheap and too 'ugly' to sing. I hesitate to sing 'Crown him, crown him. . .'. I believe there is no need to crown him. He has been crowned already by God. Otherwise, how is the gospel possible? Don't crusade against Jesus Christ! Evangelism has not made any significant headway in Asia for the last four hundred years because Christians crusaded against Asians. When did Christianity become a cheap military campaign? Who made it so? I submit that a good hundred million American dollars, a hundred years of crusading will not make Asia Christian. Christian faith does not and cannot be spread by crusading. It will spread without money, without bishops, without theologians, without plannings, if people see a crucified mind, not a crusading mind, in Christians.

What is this crucified mind?

It is the mind of Jesus Christ. It is not a persecution complex. It is not a neurotic mind. It is not a stingy and condemning mind. It is not a paternalistic mind. It is a two-way-traffic mind. It is a mind of self-denial. It is a community-building mind. It is a mind saying, 'in dying I come to you'. It is a mind obedient to the command, 'go therefore'. If we have this mind people will see it. People are perceptive. They will ask the secret of this crucified mind. That is evangelism.

Our Christianity has become a one-way-traffic religion. Jesus Christ is not a one-way-traffic Lord. It is not people out there who need repentance. It is, first of all, we who need repentance. We are far more arrogant than people on the streets. We are bigoted. We are prestige minded. We are money minded. We want to be called 'doctor', 'bishop', 'president'. We are self-righteous. We want to teach but we do not want to learn. Christianity suffers from a 'teacher complex'. We are uglier than we think. We are becoming more and more blind because we say we can see (John 9.41).

Christianity is not identical with Jesus Christ. But Jesus Christ stands in the centre of Christianity. At the moment of our repentance we see him standing among us. 'Lo, I am with you always, to the close of the age' (Matt. 28.20). Because of this promise, the promise that brings forth our repentance, Christianity has a future.

The future belongs to those who repent. As we repent, we begin to see our neighbours, their spirituality, their frustrations, their aspirations, to which Christ is ever speaking. 'Blessed are the meek, for they shall inherit the earth' (Matt. 5.5). 'The time is fulfilled, and the Kingdom of God is at hand; repent, and believe in the gospel' (Mark 1.15).

20 Sword and Religions

Put your sword back into its place; for all who take the sword will perish
by the sword.   *Matthew 26.52*

The First World Conference on Religion and Peace (WCRP) met in Kyoto, Japan, from 16 to 21 October 1970, just after Expo 70. There were 219 delegates (97 Christians, 38 Buddhists, 23 Hindus, 19 Shintoists, 18 Muslims, 7 Jews, 3 Sikhs, 2 Zoroastrians, 1 Confucian, 1 Jain and 10 others). The Honorary President of WCRP is His Grace Kosho Ohtani, the President of the Japan Buddhist Federation. Three hundred reporters were on hand to report the proceedings to the four corners of the world. Archbishop Helder Pessoa Camara from Brazil and Dr Eugene C. Blake, General Secretary of the World Council of Churches, were there among other Christian delegates. (*Report on WCRP 1970 Kyoto*) The Second WCRP was held in Leuven, Belgium, from 28 August to 3 September 1974 with 173 delegates from nearly 50 countries. 'Drawing upon the inexhaustible resources of our several spiritual heritages, we have experienced together the truth expressed by one of the poets in our midst: "I walk on thorns, but firmly, as among flowers".' (from the *Leuven Declaration*)

There were three main agendas in Kyoto: (1) disarmament, (2) development, and (3) human rights. In the words of Dr Homer A. Jack, Secretary-General of WCRP, the WCRP is 'not primarily devoted to sermon-making. Instead, the participants spent hours and days together discussing specific issues on the world's agendas for human survival'. Indeed, these three areas are immediately related to the very survival of mankind today. The Kyoto Report opens up with this sentence: 'Armaments are a threat to world peace, a hindrance to development, and a mockery of human rights'. It rejects 'the argument of governments and groups that suggest that their own security depends on their military strength and that fear of military retaliation is a positive deterrent to war and that therefore it is the best guarantee of world peace'. It urges 'the governments of the world to undertake measures required to bring about total disarmament'.

We may not want to take such a statement as this seriously, particularly when it is made by religious people. We may say that while what is said is true, the world in which we live today is a brutal world of power and politics. Such an idea as 'total disarmament' is romantic and even irresponsible. Civilized mankind has always possessed some kind of armament.

Before I go any further, I wish to quote one long paragraph from Philip Noel-Baker:

And this is what happened on 6 August 1945 at Hiroshima: 8.15 a.m. The streets are full of people; people going to work, people going to shop, people – smaller people – going to school. It was a lovely summer morning, sunshine and blue sky. Blue sky stands for happiness in Japan. The air raid siren sounds. No one pays attention. There's only a single enemy aircraft in the sky. The aircraft flies across the city. Above the centre, something falls. It's hard to see – the bomb is very small, two kilograms in weight, a little larger than a tennis-ball in size. It falls for ten to fifteen seconds, it falls and falls. Then there is a sudden searing flash of light, brighter and hotter than a thousand suns. Those who were looking directly at it had their eyes burnt in their sockets. They never looked again on men or things. In the street below there was a business man in charge of large affairs, walking to his work. A lady, as elegant as she was beautiful. A brilliant student, the leader of his class; a little girl, laughing as she ran. And in a moment they were gone. They vanished from the earth. They were utterly consumed by the furnace of the flash. There were no ashes even on the pavement. Nothing but their black shadows on the stones. Scores of thousands more, sheltered by walls or buildings by the flash, were driven mad by an intolerable thirst that followed from the heat. They ran in frenzied hordes towards the seven rivers of the delta on which Hiroshima is built. They fought like maniacs to reach the water. If they succeeded, they stooped to drink the poisoned stream, and in a month they, too, were dead. Then came the blast, thousands of miles an hour. Buildings in all directions for kilometres, flattened to the ground. Lorries, cars, milk-carts, human beings, babies' prams, picked up and hurled like lethal projectiles, hundred of metres through the air. The blast piled its victims up in frightful heaps, seven or eight corpses deep. Then the fireball touched the earth, and scores of conflagrations, fanned by hurricane winds, joined in a fire-storm. And many thousands more, trapped by walls of flame, that leaped higher than the highest tower in the town, in swiftly or in longer agony, were burnt to death. Then all went black as night. The mushroom cloud rose to 40,000 feet. It blotted out the sun. It dropped its poison dust, its fall-out, on everything that still remained not lethal in Hiroshima. And death by radioactive sickness from the fall-out was the fate of those who had survived the flash, the river, the blast, the fire-storm.[7]

Thirty years later (6 August 1975) the science editor of the *London Times* wrote: ' . . . two hundred and forty thousand people died within an hour. Today, in Hiroshima, many young people who were only embryos in their mother's womb when the bomb fell, show the fatal seeds of leukaemia. . . . Let's remember that the Hiroshima bomb was a nuclear midget.' By 1977 the number of nuclear war-heads held by the United States and Soviet Union together reached 12,500. The total annihilating power of this supply surpasses that which devastated Hiroshima by 1.3 million times!

The post-war Constitution of Japan expresses the self-understanding of the Japanese people, how they destroyed others and destroyed themselves by waging war. Through this painful experience came *Article Nine*:

Aspiring sincerely to an international peace based on justice and order, the Japanese people forever renounce war as a sovereign right of the nation and the threat or use of force as means of settling international disputes. In order to accomplish the aim of the preceding paragraph, land, sea, and air forces, as well as other war potential, will never be maintained. The right of belligerency of the state will not be recognized.

What Jesus Christ said about the use of the sword the Japanese people said in this *Article Nine* when their nation was utterly destroyed in 1945. The new constitution was 'suggested' by the occupational powers. But studies on this subject have shown that the Japanese people were not simply subjected to this suggestion. They accepted it because they themselves thought that this article of peace must be in the new constitution. They were convinced of the great importance of this article not only for them but for the whole world. With full awareness of their responsibility and of 'the high ideals' expressed, the Japanese people consented to live their new life under this new Peace Constitution. It was promulgated on

3 November 1946 and came into effect on 3 May 1947.

So it is not just a group of religious people who speak for total disarmament. One hundred million Japanese people did so in 1946! *Article Nine* does not refer to partial disarmament. It speaks for total disarmament.

How have the Japanese people distanced themselves from this holy commitment! How quickly! On 24 March 1978, at a Foreign Affairs Committee of the Diet, the Japanese prime minister Takeo Fukuda disclosed his own interpretation of *Article Nine* according to which Japan can maintain, without violating *Article Nine*, nuclear or bacteriological weapons if they are for self-defence![8]

Nahum Goldman is president of the World Jewish Congress since 1951, former president of the World Zionist Organization and president of the Conference on Jewish Material Claims Against Germany. He is deeply involved in the unmerciful world of international power politics. Since 1948 he has lived through the hope and despair of the State of Israel. He knows the grave difficulty the creation of Israel brought to the Arab people. Yet he envisions the possibility:

> Israel at peace with the Arab world, Israeli dynamism and ingenuity, coupled with Arab talents and Arab wealth, could make out of the Middle East in a few generations one of the great centers of world civilization, as it was in the past.

Obstacles to this goal are shown in these words:

> Since the establishment of the State, however, the Arab-Israeli conflict has not been handled with statesmanship and vision, but by day-to-day, short-sighted methods. . . . This state of war, inevitably forced Israel to concentrate its great moral and intellectual resources on defending its existence and securing its survival, and led it to abandon, or rather neglect, the great historical, moral and spiritual aspects of the restoration of a Jewish state. Its leaders no longer were thinkers, idealists and revolutionaries, but technicians, managers, generals and party politicians.[9]

Nahum Goldman points out to us that often 'realistic' people are only 'technicians, managers, generals and party politicians' and they do not come to grips with the 'real' issues of mankind since they work 'skillfully' but with 'short-sighted methods'. The truth – the terrible truth the Japanese people learned in 1945 – is: 'all who take the sword will perish by the sword'. How then are we to introduce this 'far-sighted insight' into the concrete conflict situations in which the nations are involved? This is *real* politics. The 'statesman' is one who never forgets the limitation of 'sword'. Anyone who is blind about this limitation will endanger the total well-being of mankind on this planet.

The Kyoto Declaration speaks of seven common convictions:

1. The fundamental unity of the human family, and the equality and dignity of all human persons.

2. The sacredness of the individual person and his/her conscience.

3. The value of human community.

4. That human power is not self-sufficient and absolute.

5. That love, compassion, selflessness, and the forces of inner truthfulness and of the spirit have ultimately a greater power than human hate, enmity and self-interest.

6. The obligation to stand by the side of the poor and the oppressed as against the rich and the oppressors.

7. That good will finally prevail.

These are human convictions, full of 'human contents'. They are not particularly religious convictions. It is imperative for us to live with the awareness of such 'human contents'. Militarism, in great and small scales, is the power that tries to destroy these 'human contents'. In today's world Jesus' words on the sword have special importance. It is a warning directed to the heart of humanity's existence. We may disappear from this planet if we do not take these words seriously. They are not abstract. They are words we can and do experience in our life.

21   Silence Towards Word

> He was oppressed, and he was afflicted, yet he opened not his mouth; like a lamb that is led to the slaughter, and like a sheep that before its shearers is dumb, so he opened not his mouth.   *Isaiah 53.7*

The Buddhist legend tells us that after Gotama Siddhattha achieved Enlightenment and thus became the Buddha (the Enlightened One) he pondered whether he should preach the truth he had discovered. Here is a stanza:

> Must I now preach what I so hardly won?
> Men sunk in sin and lusts would find it hard

to plumb this Doctrine, – up stream all the way.
Abstruse, profound, most subtle, hard to grasp.
Dear lusts will blind them that they shall not see,
– in densest mists of ignorance befogged.[10]

But at the persistent request of Brahma Sahampati the Buddha decided to preach. His first sermon, 'The Setting in Motion of the Dhamma Wheel', was preached in the Deer Park of Isipatana (Sarnath) near Benares.

Perhaps this was the first and last doubt of the Enlightened One. Should he preach? He understood the 'abstruse, profound, most subtle, hard to grasp' reason why man suffers. He now knew the way of emancipation from the suffering. He was above all gods and men. He was the Enlightened One. He pondered. Then he decided to preach. Mankind owes a great debt to Brahma Sahampati. We must realize how fortunate we are that the Buddha chose the word instead of silence. He knew the difficulty involved more than we do. Think of the contents of the communication. Elimination of greed. He knew that the difficulty was not just a matter of the art of preaching or of the formulation of his doctrine or of the clarity of his philosophical construction. The difficulty was that man lives 'in densest mists of ignorance befogged'. It is an ignorance that does not understand the destructiveness of human greed. Man lives in greed. To them the Buddha decided to preach . . . after he pondered.

The Buddha spoke. He taught us that *avijja* (ignorance) produces *tanha* (greed) and tanha produces *dukkha* (suffering). These three words are of great importance for Buddhism. They stand in a relationship of 'Conditional Arising'. If there is ignorance then greed is bound to come, if greed is there then suffering is bound to come. Then if there is suffering it comes from greed, and if there is greed that must have come from ignorance. The Buddha spoke on this Conditional Arising. . . . He thought that this doctrine is 'abstruse, profound, most subtle, hard to grasp'. Perhaps we do not think so. We may think this doctrine is quite easy to understand. It is simply one kind of conditionalism, we may say. True, but how many of us understand this from the 'inside'? We may understand it in our head. But we may not understand it with all our personal existence. How many of us really try to get rid of ignorance? Not an ordinary kind of ignorance, but the ignorance that inspires greed? Do we, in short, really put up a life-and-death struggle against the power of blind greed that is within us?

The Buddha decided to speak. This decision is contributive to the culture of humanity. I understand that the fundamental silence – decision to non-communication – is negative to human culture.

Buddhism has the doctrine of *pratyekabuddha* (Private Buddha) or Buddha who has found his enlightenment yet refuses to preach. Such a Buddha is negative and egoistic and lacks the posture of a positive participation in human culture. What is the value of wisdom if one decides not to speak about it?

God speaks. God has spoken. God will speak. . . . Jesus Christ spoke. I don't think he was a talkative person. But I am sure that he was not *pratyekabuddha* type. He spoke for the benefit of man. He spoke the Word that was from the beginning. He spoke as the Word that was from the beginning. He did indeed say a few words even on the cross. He was not silent. He was sincerely dedicated to communication. Yet . . . at times he remained silent.

> Then Pilate said to him, 'Do you not hear how many things they testify against you?' But he gave him no answer, not even to a single charge; so that the governor wondered greatly (Matt. 27.13,14).

Jesus did not say one word for his own defence. Why did he remain silent? Was he himself not the Word and Communication? If I were there I would feel the same as the governor felt.

Matthew 27.13,14 stands in the spiritual tradition of Isaiah 53.7: 'He was oppressed, and he was afflicted, yet he opened not his mouth; like a lamb that is led to the slaughter, and like a sheep that before its shearers is dumb, so he opened not his mouth.' He did not open his mouth. But he spoke. He spoke not through his mouth. He spoke through his life. He spoke through his total personality, his total commitment, his total spiritual energy and his total love for others. He did not speak by his mouth. He remained silent and 'the governor wondered greatly'. The verb here used connotes the sense of awe in the presence of the supernatural. He spoke through life – that is the language of love.

I am grateful to both Gotama the Buddha and Jesus the Christ. Both of them communicated to us of their innermost mind. Silence must be placed towards Word. Silence placed towards Silence is ultimately meaningless. Word placed towards Silence is again ultimately meaningless. 'In the beginning was the Word. . . . ' (John 1.1). 'That which was from the beginning, which we have heard, which we have seen with our eyes, which we have looked upon and touched with our hands, concerning the word of life – . . . so that you may have fellowship with us; and our fellowship is with the Father and with his Son Jesus Christ. And we are writing this that our joy may be complete. . . . ' (I John 1.1).

22   Parochial Truth is Deceptive

. . . and you will know the truth, and the truth will make you free.
John 8.32

. . . Yes, what is the word? . . . *parochial* mentality.

What a word! It comes from the word *parish*. It means the mind restricted to a small and narrow scope. It is the mind which does not go beyond its own familiar 'parish'. This is our problem today.

Today? . . . Don't you know we travel a lot? Look at Japan Air Lines, Cathay Pacific, Qantas, Thai International, . . . flying with full loads of people in all directions at 600 miles an hour. How about train and bus services which are connecting cities and remote parts of countries. Going beyond our own parish is the dominant characteristic or practical pastime of our day. Dynamic mobility stands at the centre of our life. We hear radio. We come to know through our 10 dollar radio what is happening at the Montreal Olympics, about Mars, 213 million miles away, and a Japanese ex-Prime Minister who was jailed on account of receiving bribery of US $1.6 million from the American Lockheed Corporation. We have telephone, telegram, television, airmail, newspapers, paper-back books, movies. . . . If we don't travel ourselves our media are travelling for us. We know so much about the world beyond our own 'parish'. We are not restricted to a narrow scope. If anything we are not parochial. We are very well informed.

Congratulations! Yet, mobility and communication do not heal our parochial mentality. Parochial mentality derives from a lack of imagination in our spirituality. It is not a geographical concept. One can be parochial after going around the world ten times lecturing on international relationship for ten years and while surrounded by three sets of colour televisions and driving two Datsuns. Parochial mentality is a spiritual malady. If it were not so, it could be healed easily. It is a spirituality of self-centred search for security, the spirit of self-admiration, prejudice and one-way-traffic.

Have you seen a film called 'One Flew Over the Cuckoo's Nest'? A pretty powerful film. How would you like to be working with that head nurse? I just cannot imagine how any human community can breath oxygen when watched with that kind of look. She must be a well trained nurse. A registered psychiatric nurse? In spite of her training (including group therapy technique) she does not show any understanding of the most fundamental wish of her charges. A person wants to be treated as a person. The holiness of human person is located at this point. Human relationship is human-dignity-relationship. She must be extensively travelled, to use the image already used, in the world of her profession, but she is destructively parochial. An irony that the experts are expert in their field, but blind about the basic *living* truth about human dignity and freedom cuts through this movie. Inmates of the mental institution live much closer to the basic issue of human life and have first hand experience of it. What an intriguing plot indeed.

The head nurse represents the institution. She enjoys her responsible 'institutional position' by rigidly applying to the patients 'institutionally formulated truth' about them. 'The truth will make you free' (John 8.32). But in this film this 'institutionally formulated truth' has not made anyone free. Despair and suffering are the companions of all the people concerned. As important and helpful to us as institutions are, they can impoverish and even destroy our life. In the film, institutionally formulated truth was a parochial truth. It beats around the bushes in sophisticated, logical language but it has not been electrified by the truth which will make man free.

Parochial truth destroys man. Truth which is parochial is a sick truth – more than that – it is a poisonous truth. Parochial truth then is not truth; because truth, if it is truth, 'will make you free'. The truth which makes man unfree, enslaved, impoverished, despaired, must not be the truth to which John is bearing witness. Parochial truth is a truth which is subservient to the interest, prestige and security of the 'parish' people among whom it is born.

Parochial truth is deceptive. A good example of it is given in Jeremiah; 'Do not trust in these deceptive words; "This is the temple of the Lord, the temple of the Lord, the temple of the Lord" ' (7.4). Jeremiah attacked the Jerusalem bound parochial truth. The city of God became the centre of parochial self-admiration truth. The temple was demolished by the truth that will make man free. Recently (July 1976) seven New Zealanders who believed in white racial supremacy joined the Rhodesian army. They declared themselves to be racists. Racism is a violent parochialism. It is of demonically narrow scope. That there are races in one human species is a truth. But when this truth is made parochial it becomes racism.

How to battle against this venomous king cobra, parochial mentality? It is to train ourselves to live not just in human relationship but in human-dignity-relationship. Here we need all the great resources of our faith. In faith we see that God inspires us for this (Gen. 2.7). For this Christ gave his life. For this the Holy Spirit comes to us. The breath of life is not a parochial breath. The death

of Christ is not a parochial death. The inspiration of the Holy Spirit
is not a parochial inspiration (Acts 2).

23   What is Syncretism?

Therefore God has highly exalted him and bestowed on him the name
which is above every name, that at the name of Jesus every knee should
bow, in heaven and on earth and under the earth, and every tongue confess
that Jesus Christ is Lord, to the glory of God the Father.
                                                   Philippians 2.9–11

This word *syncretism* derives from the Greek *synkretizein* meaning
'to make two parties join against a third'. The term originally
signified a political alliance. The Dutch humanist Erasmus of the
sixteenth century latinized the word giving it the meaning of an
eclectic mixture in philosophical and theological doctrines. A syncretic Christianity would be, for instance, a Christianity mixed with
Buddhism.

Even without any suggestion of mixing, the question of the meaning of religion is a formidable one. How, then, the religions mix
with each other, influence each other or penetrate each other is a
greatly complicated question to answer. Syncretism is abhorred by
many Christians often for too simple a grasp of the issue involved.

Here is a Thai person. He was born in Thailand where his father,
grandfather and great grandfather were born. He speaks the Thai
language. Generation after generation his family and their neighbours have spoken this language. He is a Buddhist just as most of
his country people are. His language and thoughts are deeply
influenced by the doctrine and practice of Buddhism. His emotion,
his psychological life, is strongly coloured by the Buddhist outlook.
His community is also a Buddhist community. Certain days are
held to be sacred according to the Buddhist calendar.

One day this man, who lives in a predominantly Buddhist culture,
becomes a Christian. He will naturally bring his Buddhist way of
thinking, emotion and outlook into the new faith. His mother culture, like his mother tongue, is Buddhistic. He will speak about his
new faith with the words of his mother tongue and the accent of his
mother culture. But the American missionary also, even after twenty

years residence in Japan, speaks his adopted language, Japanese, with the accent and formulations of his mother tongue, English. And that is not an impoverishment of the Japanese culture but on the contrary, a positive enrichment. He is bringing something new and exciting to the Japanese language and culture by using the Japanese language in a new way.

Shall we say that our Thai man must not bring his Buddhist background to the new faith in Christ? Must he be purged, or purified of his essential nature? I find this too abstract. He has 'lived' for seven centuries under strong Buddhist persuasion and culture and cannot suddenly 'purify' himself of its influence any more than a European could separate himself from the Christian influence. The mother culture, like the mother tongue, will follow a person throughout life. He wears it as he wears his skin.

The Christian faith, expressed powerfully in every page of the New Testament, also speaks with the accent of the mother culture, Judaism. '. . . there cannot be any such thing, as the *ecclesia pura*, the non-mediated Church, the non-translated truth and doctrine – a Christianity chemically pure, so to speak, and in a non-adapted form.'[11] God is not 'chemically pure' as long as he calls himself the 'God of Abraham, Isaac and Jacob'. He is in contact with people and he allows himself to be introduced by quoting three human names. The loving God of the covenant and the chemically pure God cannot be reconciled. Jesus Christ is not 'chemically pure'. 'As the Father has sent me, even so I send you' says the risen Lord (John 20.21). That the 'Father has sent me' is Jesus' basic personal identity. The Father sent him all the way from 'Bethlehem to Golgotha'.

'This man receives sinners and eats with them'! (Luke 15.2)

He spoke the Galilean Aramaic, a very specific language. He never spoke English, French, Japanese or German. The New Testament was not written in Galilean Aramaic but in *koine* Greek, the common nonliterary Greek of the times. Jesus used parables and images which were taken out of his own time and his own culture. He never mentioned the Buddha or Confucius. He lived in a definite place, within a definite culture and used his mother's language. He was not 'pure' in the sense that he kept himself from involving in a concrete culture and history. The *incarnation* – the Word which 'became flesh' was the *in-culturation* for it 'dwelt among us' (John 1.14).

Culture, like language, is a continuous reality. Chinese culture and language reaches back four thousand years; the Japanese two thousand years. And culture is a process in which there is much bringing of 'gifts' from other cultures and religions. No culture is pure. No history, no religion, no language, no race, no philosophy is 'pure'. There are only interactions, adaptations, assimilations, integrations and disintegrations. Culture is the process of reception-rejection.

So our Thai man brings his Buddhist background into his new faith in Jesus Christ. Thai Buddhism, as well as the Judaeo-Christian Old Testament, says 'thou shalt not commit adultery'. This concept, then, will be easily understood and assimilated in his new religion.

Frequently the Buddhist teaching is summarized in the brief stanza:

> Cease to do evil,
> Learn to do good
> Purify your own mind.

I am sure that there will be no clash between this understanding and the new faith of our Thai man. Who would ask him to reject such a noble heritage of Buddhism when he becomes a Christian? I cannot imagine that Jesus Christ dislikes this stanza.

Thai Buddhists support the temples and monasteries by their own giving. They are trained to give. To take away from him the simple, loving giving from his own substance and his own table would be rather an impoverishment than an enrichment of the life of our Thai man.

But how about this?

> To the Buddha I go for refuge.
> To the Dhamma (teaching) I go for refuge.
> To the Sangha (order of monks) I go for refuge.

These are central affirmations of Buddhists. Can they come into the new faith of our Thai Christian? He used to say 'To the Buddha I go for refuge'. Now he says, 'To Jesus I go for refuge'. Can he say both? Can he say 'The Buddha is my salvation *and* Jesus Christ is my salvation'? The Buddha has taught him many noble and good things. In what sense does he remain to be his salvation? He cannot say, surely, that salvation in Buddha is identical with salvation in Jesus Christ. Both of them stand for salvation, but now he is convinced and believes in Jesus Christ as the ultimate salvation for him. His turning to the Buddha for refuge must in some way change. Still he may have a grateful memory of how the Buddha nourished him spiritually before he came to Jesus Christ.

'God is our refuge and strength, a very present help in trouble' (Ps. 46.1). The concept of taking refuge in the source of his salvation is part of the Thai man's heritage. His spiritual training in this will be a great asset as he begins his new spiritual life in Jesus Christ.

Or would it be a hindrance? He is syncretic only if he insists that the salvation in Buddha and Jesus Christ are identical. If he is able to distinguish the gifts of his heritage and his new faith his attitude will not be syncretic but responsible and discerning. His life will be greatly enriched.

Paul was a Pharisee. He had a spiritual as well as an academic training in this great tradition. In his letter to the Philippians Paul reviews his life; '. . . circumcised on the eighth day, of the people of Israel, of the tribe of Benjamin, a Hebrew born of Hebrew; as to the law a Pharisee, as to zeal a persecutor of the church, as to righteousness under the law blameless' (3.5,6). He continues, telling what happened to all this great personal prestige and advantage when he became a Christian. 'But whatever gain I had, I counted as loss for the sake of Christ. Indeed I count everything as loss because of the surpassing worth of knowing Christ Jesus my Lord. For his sake I have suffered the loss of all things, and count them as refuse, . . . ' (3.7,8).

Yet, I am sure that Paul was able to make use of his Pharisaic training if not his Pharisaic attitude or conviction, for the glory of the Messiah, Jesus Christ. He was able to baptize it and make good use of it in the new context of life in Jesus. Krister Stendahl observes that it is 'achievement' orientation and achievement-based-security that he now thinks of as refuse.[12] The name of Jesus Christ does not stand for demolition or 'scorched land bombing'. He did not destroy everything of my former education and formation when I came to him. After I became a Christian I still lived in the cultural world of Japan. I worship Christ with the emotion and thought which derives from the culture of Japan. I am led to believe that Jesus Christ inspires me to find out ways in which I can make use of my Japanese heritage. I, who was born in the Japanese culture, who wear Japanese-ness with my skin, am re-receiving my own culture. It is not experience of demolition but of resurrection. The Thai man will worship Christ with the spirit trained in 'taking refuge in Buddha'. Thus he will bring to Jesus his own adoration as a Thai man.

In Jesus Christ, then, is the principle of the ecumenical movement. '. . . at the name of Jesus every knee should bow, in heaven and on earth and under the earth' (Phil. 2.10). The ecumenical movement is to bring all cultural, religious, linguistic, ethnically conditioned doxologies to Jesus Christ.

Is there, then, no such thing as syncretism? There is. When we bring all to bow at the name of Jesus we are not syncretic. But if we place the name of Jesus with any other name and say that there is really no difference between it and the other names we become syncretic. Bringing our religious customs and orientations to his presence is not syncretic. It is an ecumenical movement. Such an ecumenical movement is a spiritually awakened one. It is an exciting spiritual and culturally refreshing experience. One should see his own culture blessed and enriched.

24   Grey Hairs and the People of Other Faith

> Hearken to me, O house of Jacob, all the remnant of the house of Israel, who have been borne by me from your birth, carried from the womb; even to your old age I am He, and to grey hairs I will carry you. I have made, and I will bear; I will carry and will save.   *Isaiah 46.3,4*

We are today living in a world in which the great historic religious traditions are encountering each other. The Wheaton Congress, convened in April 1966, takes up the subject of syncretism. Harold Lindsell writes about the Congress' view on syncretism:

> If the other religions of the world are truly saving vehicles, and if men are redeemed while in those religions, the gospel is neither final nor unique. If salvation is to be found in Hinduism, which denies the personhood of God, the theism of the Bible is an errant viewpoint. If Jainism, which lacks a supreme personal deity, is a saving religion, Christianity's God is unnecessary. If Buddhism, which was originally atheistic and is still decidedly a religion of fundamental impersonalism, is efficacious, Christianity has lost its real genius. If Sikhism and Mohammedanism, which are unitarian in their views of deity, are saving religions, the Trinity and the person of Jesus have been robbed of their biblical significance. If Confucianism, which lacks a supreme personal deity, can bring men to eternal life and the forgiveness of sins, Calvary and Christ's atonement by blood have no particular validity. If Shinto with its heterogeneous polytheism is adequate, what is the need for Christianity with its strong judgment against polytheism and idolatry; and who would choose stronger and more particularistic teachings when a simpler and less onerous system leads to similar results with fewer demands? Zoroastrianism, which is closer to Christianity than most of the other non-Christian religions, is still polytheistic. If it is sufficient

to meet the true spiritual needs of men when the rigidly mon-
otheistic faith of Christianity asks more, who would buy the
higher in cost when the lower would give the same results? . . .
Scripture condemns theological syncretism and declares all other
religions to be idolatry. All the gods, ideas, and religious activities
of the non-Christian religions lie under divine judgment. They
cannot save, however good the intentions of their devotees may
be and however sincere their efforts.[13]

This is a strong clear-cut view. It is the view of the Congress
representing more than 13,000 North American missionaries.
According to this view Hinduism, Jainism, Buddhism, Sikhism,
Mohammedanism, Confucianism and Zoroastrianism are 'idolatry'
and 'under divine judgment'. Christianity, yes, Christianity alone
does not stand under divine judgment.

The Indian people do not call their religion 'Hinduism'. They
call it 'The Hindu Way of Life' (the title of the one of the books by
Sarvepalli Radhakrishnan) rooted in the *sanatana dharma*, 'eternal
law'. It is interesting to notice that all these *isms* cited in the
paragraph quoted were given their names in the nineteenth century
by Westerners. W. C. Smith investigated the history of all these
religion-isms and came up with this result; Boudhism (1801) Hin-
dooism (1829) Taouism (1839) Zoroastrianism (1854) Confucianism (1862) Shintoism (1894). With Islam the history is slightly
more complicated; Mahumetisme (1597), Mahumetanism (1612),
Islamism (1747) Musulamanisme (1818).[14] These names, then,
were given by outsiders. The most complex reality of religious
thoughts and practices were neatly packaged and labelled 'so-and-
so-ism'. Such treatment is certainly useful for the outsider. It
reduces the complicated and elusive religious worlds to manageable
controlled units. Boxed-in-religions are not particularly difficult to
describe, even to making 'penetrating' comments. But living religion
cannot be contained in these boxes.

The seven religions mentioned in the quotation comprise, in total,
approximately 1,425,000,000 people according to the *Historical
Atlas of the Religions of the World*.[15] If we believe that Jesus Christ
died for these millions of people, then we must be careful what we
say about them, as Jesus Christ, who died for them, would be very
careful. Perhaps it is easy for us, who do not give our life for them,
to say sweeping things about them. All of us become suddenly
wisdom-full and penetrating when we come to make negative comments about something or someone, particularly about someone's
religion.

I try to think concretely about 35,000,000 people in the kingdom of Thailand. But I cannot think concretely about 35,000,000 people. It is impossible. So I must be modest. I am thinking of the Buddhist people I came to know in and around city of Chiengmai, in North Thailand. 'If Buddhism which was originally atheistic and is still decidedly a religion of fundamental impersonalism, is efficacious, Christianity has lost its real genius.' 'Scripture declares all other religions to be idolatry.' How am I to understand this in relation to the Thai *people* that I know?

What a distance there is between these theories of religion and the real people.

The cross of Christ inspires me to mediate on the love of God. '. . . even to your old age I am He, and to grey hairs I will carry you. I have made, and I will bear; I will carry and will save.' The love of God towards all of humanity is substantiated by this determination of God to carry us. I understand that this holy determination of God is directed to my Thai neighbours, each one of them in and around the city of Chiengmai. God is concerned about the Buddhist and all other people of whatever faith. His love is directed to the living person. There is a difference between Buddhism and Buddhist as much as 'wife-ism' and real wife who is a living person. Buddhist is a far more dynamic reality than Buddhism defined in the textbook of religions.

If Buddhism . . . is efficacious, . . .   Naturally the sentence begins with reference to the boxed-in-religion, Buddhism. The Buddha worked in a historically different world from that of Israel which was confronted by the God of Abraham, Isaac and Jacob. He lived in a geographically and culturally different world. His world was full of all kinds of gods. The Buddha neither denied nor affirmed them. Confucius, the other great sage of Asia, took a similar attitude towards the gods. The Buddha thought he had much more serious subjects to think about. The Buddha concentrated on the subject of human suffering and how to free oneself from it. Confucius focused his attention on the construction of moral orderliness (*jen*) in the human community. They could be called 'atheistic' in the same sense that Socrates in Athens was accused of being atheistic. Paul went through a somewhat similar experience. 'Men, you know that from this business we have our wealth. And you see and hear that not only at Ephesus but almost throughout all Asia this Paul has persuaded and turned away a considerable company of people, saying that gods made with hands are not gods' (Acts 19.25,26). To the Ephesians Paul was 'atheistic'. He offended the people who made a business of 'gods made with hands'. The Buddha and Confucius also offended the people who worshipped all kinds of gods. Gods were unimportant so far as they were concerned. I am happy to know that they were 'atheistic' in that sense.

But the theology reflecting the spirit of the Congress implies that the Buddha or Buddhism is 'atheistic' in the sense of the Christian usage of the term. Such observation is hasty and unfair. It does not reflect the mind of the crucified Lord. It is 'bulldozing' instead of loving and suffering. Christians must meditate on Matthew 27. 27–31 every time when they wish to say something about the men of other living faiths:

> Then the soldiers of the governor took Jesus into the praetorium, and they gathered the whole battalion before him. And they stripped him and put a scarlet robe upon him, and plaiting a crown of thorns they put it on his head, and put a reed in his right hand. And kneeling before him they mocked him, saying, 'Hail, King of the Jews!' And they spat upon him, and took the reed and struck him on the head. And when they had mocked him, they stripped him of the robe, and put his own clothes on him, and led him away to crucify him.

In the living situation of spitting and spat upon do we act the role of the governor's soldier or of Jesus?

In the Christian world the term 'atheism' means, loosely, the view that denies the existence of the *Christian* God. Behind this is an idea that 'theism' is more Christian than 'atheism'. Atheism is in direct conflict with Christianity whereas theism is not. I maintain that the crucified Lord is a scandal equally to both atheist and theist. A theist is as far from Jesus Christ as an atheist. Jesus Christ does not fit into the scheme of either theism or atheism. 'We preach Christ crucified, a stumbling block to Jews and folly to Gentiles' (I Cor. 1.23). It is no easier for the theist to accept the gospel than for an atheist. The missionary is challenged in his proclamation of the name of Christ as he is confronted by the theistic Mahayana Buddhist and the atheistic Theravada Buddhist. Jesus Christ is a stumbling block to both capitalist and communist, both white and black, both Western civilization and Eastern civilization, both Buddhist and Muslims both Christian and Jew. 'For God has consigned all men to disobedience, that he may have mercy upon all' (Rom. 11.32).

What kind of God is he? ' . . . to grey hairs I will carry you . . .'

I ask myself a question: If I take an atheistic position what does it mean?

(a) Does it mean that I say to myself that there is no god or no gods? Then the answer is quite obvious without any difficulty. I became 'an atheist' when I became a Christian.

(*b*) Does it mean that if I say to myself that there is no God of the Bible, then the God will disappear and be reduced to nothing? I would welcome such God to disappear. God who is dependent upon my view of either atheism or theism, such an undernourished God had better go quickly.

(*c*) Does it mean that Christ came to man in order to make us theists instead of atheists? For what a superficial purpose did he come!

(*d*) Does it mean that in taking an atheistic position I deny the centre of the whole Christian message? I do not recall that I became a Christian and was baptized because I was impressed by the teaching that there is a god or are many gods. This could not impress me since I come from a culture of many gods. I became a Christian because I came to know that God loves man, including me, through Jesus Christ. 'God is' does not mean too much to me. 'God loves' is more fundamental to me. What is the use of knowing that God exists if I do not know anything about his character? His love overwhelms me, only then I come to know he is. *He is* comes to me as I realize he loves me in Jesus Christ. God touches me quite apart from my inclination towards atheism or theism.

'Atheism' is a convenient word. The other ism-word used in the sentence relating to Buddhism is 'impersonalism'. One thing clear about the religion called Buddhism is that the founder must have left a very personal impression upon the people around him. The study of Buddhism, both Theravada and Mahayana schools, shows this. The following story illustrates the impression he imprinted upon his followers:

> . . . These miscreants followed the Master about the city shouting all kinds of abuse such as, 'You are a thief, an idiot, an ass. You will go to hell, you have no chance of salvation,' and so on. The Venerable Ananda, the Buddha's constant companion, was hurt when he saw the Teacher being molested publicly like that, so he spoke to the Buddha, 'Sir, these citizens are reviling us openly. Let us go elsewhere!'
>
> 'Where shall we go?' the Buddha inquired, and the following discussion ensued.
>
> 'To some other city, Sir.'
>
> 'If the people abuse us there, where shall we go?'
>
> 'To yet another city, Sir.'
>
> 'If men revile us there also, then?'
>
> 'To still another city, Sir.'
>
> 'No, Ananda, that is not the proper way. Where a difficulty arises, right there it should be resolved. Only when that is done

should one move. Rather, Ananda, I am like a battle elephant whose duty it is to withstand the arrows that are shot from all directions. Even so it is my duty to endure with patience the vile words of wicked men. This will continue only for a week and then the people will know.'[16]

This story must have been written about him by one of the circle of followers who came under the strong influence of this man, the Buddha. The stories about the Buddha which are told from generation to generation are deeply personal and moving ones. The monastic life in the Theravada countries is not 'impersonal'. The basic 227 Injunctions for the *Sangha* are very personal injunctions. The Mahayana development gives even a stronger orientation towards the coming of the personal Messiah Buddha to man. Think of the image of the *Bodhisattva*.

'If Buddhism, which was originally atheistic and is still decidedly a religion of fundamental impersonalism, is efficacious, Christianity has lost its real genius.' Don't worry, Christianity does not and cannot lose its real genius by such a feeble proposition. The God of the Bible is much stronger. The crucified and risen Lord, not 'the theism of the Bible' cannot be destroyed by such a piece of abstract definition. With Paul we believe that 'the foolishness of God is wiser than men, and the weakness of God is stronger than men' (I Cor. 1.25). God who loves man in the crucified and risen Lord does not stand under a simple formula of the Aristotelian law of contradiction. 'He died for sinners' (Rom. 5.6–8) means the coming of new possibility by the power of love. This love breaks through our egocentric thought and self-admiration formulations.

Scripture does not declare *all* other religions than Christianity to be idolatry. Scripture first of all warns that idolatry takes place within Israel and the church. Idolatry is possible in the tradition which makes the distinction between God and idols. In the traditions which do not have this distinction, in the view of such adherents, there cannot be idolatry in the Christian sense.

Scripture does not mention the word 'religion'. There is not one word about Buddhism and Hinduism, for instance. Scripture is not directing its attention to religions. It speaks to the living men in all times and in all cultures. In the light of Jesus Christ Christianity can be judged as idolatrous as any other religion. There is a difference between Christianity and Jesus Christ. 'For the time has come for judgment to begin with the household of God' (I Peter 4.17). The question of idolatry is not primarily directed to other 'religions' but to Christianity first.

When we speak about the people of other historic faiths – Hinduism, Jainism, Buddhism, Sikhism, Mohammedanism, Zoroastrianism – as cited in the quotation – let us remember the words of Isaiah – 'God who carries us'. In communion with such a faithful and loving God, let our thought be judged and illumined. . . . Then we may be able to carry a more meaningful Christian message to the *people* of the other faiths.

25   From Hostility to Hospitality

He is before all things, and in him all things hold together.
Colossians 1.17

Jesus Christ is not a Methodist. He is not an Anglican. He is not a Presbyterian. He is not a Roman Catholic. He is not an Orthodox. He is more than all of these. He is the source-person from whom all these historic traditions came to be. The source-person cannot be confined to any tradition. He works and expresses himself through these traditions, but he is free from them because he is 'the source of eternal salvation' (Heb. 5.9). That he is the source means he is 'ecumenical'. 'Where two or three are gathered in my name, there am I in the midst of them' (Matt. 18.20). Wherever, in the whole *inhabited world* (*oecumene*), two or three are gathered *in the name of Jesus Christ*, there *he is*. The source-person is 'ecumenically there'. This is the meaning of the word 'ecumenical'. 'He is before all things, and in him all things hold together.' The primacy of Jesus Christ is the foundation of the ecumenical movement.

Different churches (denominations) have come to be during the long history of Christianity. There must have been reasons for these developments at certain moments of history. But denominations are valuable and helpful *only* when they point us to Jesus Christ, the source-person of salvation. They cannot point to Jesus Christ in his wholeness and primacy unless they transcend the boundaries of their denominational security, glory and prestige. 'Then Jesus told his disciples, "If any man would come after me, let him deny himself and take up his cross and follow me" ' (Matt. 16.24).

Whether we like it or not we are living increasingly in an international, intercultural and interreligious world. Our life is constantly sandwiched between that which is *familiar* and that which is *unfamiliar*. The Japanese language to my ear is familiar, but the Thai language is unfamiliar. Christianity is familiar but Islam is unfamiliar. Japanese food is familiar but Indonesian food is unfamiliar. We feel hospitable to the person who is familiar, but hostile to one who is a stranger. Are you a Methodist? The Methodist church is familiar to you. You feel at home in it. But the Lutheran church is unfamiliar to you. You may not feel at home in it. Will you, then, just sit down all your life in your familiar corner in comfort? We must move from hostility to hospitality. We must move from the familiar to the unfamiliar. There is no other way today. Only in this movement is there hope for the survival of humankind. 'You shall not wrong a stranger or oppress him, for you were strangers in the land of Egypt' (Exod. 22.21).

The movement from hostility. to hospitality, from the fear of unfamiliarity to the joy of familiarity – this is the 'ecumenical' movement. This movement is the movement of Jesus Christ. 'For he is our peace, who has made us both one, and has broken down the dividing wall of hostility, by abolishing in his flesh the law of commandments and ordinances, that he might create in himself one new man in place of the two, so making peace, and might reconcile us both to God in one body through the cross, thereby bringing the hostility to an end' (Eph. 2.14–16). The movement between the unfamiliar and the familiar is called the movement of love. If we just stay in our familiar zones, love becomes weak from lack of exercise.

> For though I am free from all men, I have made myself a slave to all, that I might win the more. To the Jews I became as a Jew, in order to win Jews; to those under the law I became as one under the law – though not being myself under the law – that I might win those under the law. To those outside the law I became as one outside the law – not being without law toward God but under the law of Christ – that I might win those outside the law. To the weak I became weak, that I might win the weak. I have become all things to all men, that I might by all means save some. I do it all for the sake of the gospel, that I may share in its blessings.   (I Cor. 9.19–23)

> And as he sat at table in his house, many tax collectors and sinners were sitting with Jesus and his disciples; for there were many who followed him. And the scribes of the Pharisees, when they saw that he was eating with sinners and tax collectors, said to his disciples, 'Why does he eat with tax collectors and sinners?' And when Jesus heard it, he said to them, 'Those who are well have no need of a physician, but those who are sick; I came not to call the righteous, but sinners.'   *Mark 2.15–17*

'The secular' means 'this world'. Latin *saeculum*, century, age, epoch came to mean *world*. 'Secular' is an important word. It has, in itself, no negative meaning. It points to the world in which we live. We are all in the world. We are all secular. 'I do not pray that thou shouldst take them out of the world, but that thou shouldst keep them from the evil one', Jesus prays for his disciples (John 17.15). 'For God so loved the world that he gave his only Son, that whoever believes in him should not perish but have eternal life' (John 3.16). This world to which God sent his Son is the object of the love of God. In the Catholic Church 'secular priests' are the priests who live in the world and work for the people in the parishes. They are in the world, secular, but they are not 'secularist'. Jesus Christ was a secular priest. 'And as he sat at table in his house, many tax collectors and sinners were sitting with Jesus.' He was in the world. But he was not 'secularist'. An awareness of his involvement in the world alone does not make one a secularist.

The secularist is a believer in 'this-world-ism' in the sense that all human value is located within this world. He places exclusive emphasis on this world and rejects the being of a 'God who so loved the world'. 'Here' receives a decisive preeminence over 'beyond'. There is for him no connection between 'here' and 'beyond'. 'Here' does not receive interpretation from 'beyond' and *vice versa*. Reinhold Niebuhr writes in his preface to *Beyond Tragedy*: 'It is the thesis of these pages that the biblical view of life is dialectical because it affirms the meaning of history and of man's natural existence on the one hand, and on the other insists that the centre, source and fulfilment of history lie beyond history.'[17] Niebuhr's thesis would make no sense to the secularist.

To be secularist, however, is not as easy as we may think. We sense, almost unconsciously, that the 'here' stands in the shadow of the 'beyond'. This is suggested by the amazing Deuteronomy passage: ' . . . man does not live by bread alone, but by everything that proceeds out of the mouth of the Lord' (8.3). In this passage 'here' (bread) and 'beyond' (the word of God) come together to man. They cannot be separated so easily.

On 28 May 1978, there was an opening ceremony of the Narita International Airport outside of Tokyo. Construction of the airport took twelve years because of massive local opposition to government's high-handedness in pushing the project. The ceremony was conducted by Shinto priests and it was called *shin ji* (the matter of the gods). There were a sacred sword and a mirror on the altar. A Shinto convocation was said and a ritual of purification was given. While this was being done, 10,000 mobile riot control policemen were guarding the airport. Mr Fukunaga, the minister of transportation said: 'The baby born with difficulty will grow up healthily. This is an old saying. I pray that this baby too will have a strong and healthy life.' The word 'pray' is a frequently used word in Japan. It belongs to the vocabulary of the 'beyond'. Why build an altar and conduct a ceremony of purification? Why should the thought of the 'sacred' enter the airport equipped with the most sophisticated scientific gadgets? The bridge between Honshu and Kyushu and nuclear power plants in Japan have been opened in similar manner by the Shinto priests. Some kind of 'beyond' is inseparable from 'here'.

Even so, some people are secularists while others are not. This world is a puzzling world. Secularism is a puzzling *ism*. Even just 'here' is puzzling. And 'beyond' is also puzzling. But when 'here' and 'beyond' are placed together to give and receive light mutually, then they begin to have meaning. Too much emphasis on 'beyond' does not and cannot help us. 'Beyond' can be presented forcefully only if we are able to present 'here' forcefully.

'The word of God' can be presented forcefully only if we are able to present 'bread' forcefully.

The importance of *this* world far exceeds the importance of *that* world in today's general mental climate. The 'here' has received much meaning from the 'beyond' in the history of religions. Religions taught us to endure the difficulty of 'here' for the promise and glory of the 'beyond'. But this 'accepted' progression has been challenged. 'The abolition of religion as the *illusory* happiness of men is a demand for their real happiness. . . . Religion is only the illusory sun about which man revolves so long as he does not revolve about himself' (Karl Marx). 'Here' must receive its meaning within the same 'here'. We must take the criticism of Marx against religion seriously since often in the history of Christianity an unhealthy imperialism of the 'beyond' against the meaning of 'here' took place.

Today there are those who say that the 'beyond' must be 'beyond' in the context of 'here'. I welcome this as a promising 'religious' orientation. It means that they are searching for the possibility of an interpretation of religious truth through insight of 'the beyond within the here'. There is a difference between 'beyond within here' and simply 'here'.

Why 'beyond within here'? The reason must be the presence of the holy in this world (*saeculum*). There is a secular experience of the holy. There is *no* secular non-contact with the holy. Inescapably we are brought to a point of contact with the holy. Frequency does not matter. The point is that in secular space and secular time the possibility of encounter with the holy is hidden.

Jesus sat at table with tax collectors and sinners. These are the people that society has decided should be far distanced from the presence of the holy. They are 'unholy people', not cultured and respectable people. Jesus ate with them. Complaints come from the 'holy religious' people. In their view, Jesus, the holy man, is cheapening himself by associating with such people. But Jesus expresses the mind of the Holy God in one sentence: 'Those who are well have no need of a physician, but those who are sick; I came not to call the righteous but sinners.' ('I have not come to call respectable people, but outcasts.' TEV) He was with the tax collectors and sinners, and he said this to the people who made complaints. The tax collectors and sinners are 'secular' people. The scribes of the Pharisees were 'secularists' in the eyes of Jesus Christ. In the ordinary sense this is not so. The Pharisees are not 'secular'. They are dedicated 'religious' people. But failing to see the presence of the 'Grace from Beyond' eating with the people 'in the world', they showed themselves to be secularists. They wanted to see a separation, a distance between Jesus and the tax collectors and sinners. This is a hidden 'secularist' sentiment.

Secular is a beautiful word. In the 'secular' – this world – we may meet Jesus Christ. Where else? But 'secularist' is a pagan. He tries to separate the 'Grace from Beyond' from this world.

27   Secret Strength

Have you not known? Have you not heard? The Lord is the everlasting God, the Creator of the ends of the earth. He does not faint or grow weary, his understanding is unsearchable. He gives power to the faint, and to him who has no might he increases strength. Even youths shall faint and be weary, and young men shall fall exhausted; but they who wait for the Lord shall renew their strength, they shall mount up with wings like eagles, they shall run and not be weary, they shall walk and not faint.

Isaiah 40.28–31

On the temple bell
Perching, sleeps
The butterfly, oh.   (Buson 1716–1783)

This *haiku* takes me instantly to the quiet compound of a Buddhist temple in the mountains of Japan. I walk around in the silent, deserted compound. It is about two o'clock in the afternoon. The warm sun and the soft shades of the pine trees present a sleepy contrast. I hear in the distance the sound of a stream running against the rocks. By chance I stroll towards the temple bell-tower. Looking up to the huge iron gong I see . . . a tiny colourful butterfly on the bell . . . asleep, motionless. 'Why do you sleep there of all places?' . . . because it is quiet here. Yes. Indeed, how quiet it is. How quiet is the huge gong which is not at work. Philosopher butterfly. That which can be loudest can become quietest. This is Zen philosophy. Are you a Zen butterfly?

I have lived with this strange logic. That which can be loudest can become quietest. That which can be strongest can become weakest. That which can be wisest can become most foolish. The quality of quietude, weakness and foolishness here is different from the ordinary concept of quietude, weakness and foolishness. They are extraordinary. They suggest 'self-limitation' and 'self-denial'. Self-denial for the sake of self? Or for others? Is it egocentric self-denial or other-centred self-denial? Egocentric self-denial is sickly. Other-centred self-denial is creative. The huge gong is quiet for the sake of a small butterfly. A mother walks slowly for the sake of her child. God becomes 'weak' for the sake of man (I Cor. 1.25). Through the one who was crucified God embraces man.

God does not simply love man. That would be the love of God without secret. That would be an ordinary love of an ordinary God. When the New Testament says 'God is love' it must be revealing the extraordinary quality of the love of God to man. He comes, in fact, with the symbol of the cross. A crucified God! The strongest became weakest! For what? For himself? Did God engage in the supreme egocentric self-denial? No. He denied himself for the sake of the others. And this is the form of love and form of strength in the New Testament.

Oh, frail butterfly, what a contrast between you and the heavy mass of iron. You look so precarious and transitory against this background. Precariousness and transitoriness go together. Gotama Buddha engaged in six years of meditation on these subjects. My own life is precarious and transitory. That which is beyond precariousness and transitoriness – is that eternity? But I am not interested in an eternity which has nothing to do with transitoriness. The New Testament supports me in this. Strength is strength when it makes weak strong. Beauty is beauty when it makes not-beautiful beautiful. Wisdom is wisdom when it makes foolish wise. Love is love when it makes unlovable lovable. Righteousness is righteousness when it makes unrighteous righteous. Eternity is eternity when it makes transitoriness eternal. This eternity which makes transitoriness eternal is different from the ordinary concept of eternity. It is an eternity that embraces transitoriness. ' . . . while he was yet at a distance, his father saw him and had compassion, and ran and embraced him and kissed him' (Luke 15.20). Eternity is more than a time-concept. It is a love-concept. When love comes to transitoriness and embraces it, it is called eternity. Otherwise eternity is only an abstract concept.

Our life is very much like the butterfly in the *haiku*. Our life is not as enduring as the temple bell. 'Come now, you who say, "Today or tomorrow we will go into such and such a town and spend a year there and trade and get gain"; whereas you do not know about tomorrow. What is your life? For you are a mist that appears for a little time and then vanishes. Instead you ought to say, "If the Lord wills, we shall live and we shall do this or that" ' (James 4.13–15). Do not make yourself big. Self-enlargement is a conceited goal. If we can be rescued from this attraction, we can maintain our spiritual 'strength'. This is the possibility Isaiah is talking about. 'Even youths shall faint and be weary, and young men shall fall exhausted; but they who wait for the Lord shall renew their strength.' 'They who wait for the Lord' will be spiritually strengthened yet free from destructive self-glorification. They are restful yet full of actions. They are quiet yet committed. What a genuinely attractive and creative possibility.

Oh, the butterfly. . . . you look so trusting. You are sound sleep. You do not engage in self-enlargement. You speak of the beauty of trust and of peace. You point to the secret of spiritual strength. . . . Sometimes I feel you are inviting me to read Isaiah 40.28–31. Thank you . . .

III Nation Searching

> Judge not, that you be not judged. For with the judgment you pronounce you will be judged, and the measure you give will be the measure you get. Why do you see the speck that is in your brother's eye, but do not notice the log that is in your own eye?
> *Matthew 7.1–3*

A recent issue of a periodical in the field of law study (*Hōgaku Seminar Zōkan* February 1977, Tokyo) carries the result of a survey conducted on the subject of 'the emperor' among university students. How do the university students in Japan today see the emperor? This study was carried out during the national celebration for the fiftieth year of the reign of the present emperor in November 1976. The survey took two weeks. 1700 university students in the Tokyo area were contacted.

Here are some of the significant results.

What do you think is the best symbol for Japan and for the unity of the Japanese people? (1423 responded)

Rice	1.5%
Cherry Tree	10.5
Dove	2.0
Emperor	9.1
Mount Fuji	10.5
Rising Sun National Flag	18.1
National Anthem	0.5
Crown Princess	0.4
Others	5.1
No need for the symbol	32.5
Do not understand	9.8

What is your feeling towards the emperor and the imperial household? (1394 responded)

Awesome and worthy to be respected	1.9%
Feel close	9.0
No feeling	60.6
Positive dislike	16.0
Others	12.5

What kind of 'being' is the emperor? (1375 responded)

God or divine person	0.4%
Not divine but someone more than the ordinary person	3.5
Ordinary person and dependable	9.3
Completely same as any ordinary Japanese person	71.9
Others	14.9

Do you think it better to have the emperor or not? (1399 responded)

Better to have him	22.0%
One way or other does not make any difference	35.2
Better not to have him	37.2
Do not understand	5.6

Do you think the emperor should be male, or in the future provision should be made that a female person could become the empress? (1419 responded)

Must be male	14.4%
Could be female	46.7
Not concerned	30.2
Other	5.5
Do not understand	3.2

Do you approve of the national celebration of the fiftieth year of the Emperor's rule sponsored by the Government? (1420 responded)

Approve	14.8%
Do not approve	52.2
Do not understand	22.1
Other	10.6

Do you think the emperor was responsible for the last war? (1403 responded)

Not responsible	9.5%
Responsible	68.4
Difficult to decide	16.5
Not concerned	1.2
Do not understand	4.4

How do you feel when you see the national flag? (1423 responded)

Inspiring	6.7%
Generally I like it	34.4

No feeling	24.1
No good feeling toward it	9.6
Positive dislike	7.1
Difficult to answer	16.5
Others	1.6

What do you think about the move towards the nationalization of the 'Yasukuni War-dead Shrine'? (1403 responded)

Approve	6.1%
Disapprove	55.7
Difficult to answer	30.6
Other	7.6

Immediately after the war an American public opinion survey by the Gallup poll indicated that 71% expressed a strongly negative attitude towards the Japanese emperor (33% favoured capital punishment, 18% were for bringing him to the War Criminal Trial, 11% for life imprisonment, 9% for exile from Japan). Only 3% supported the idea of the 'use' of the emperor for Occupational purposes.

On the other hand the survey conducted by the *Asahi Newspaper* in December 1945 revealed that only 5% of the Japanese people wanted the imperial system to be discontinued. The great majority, 78%, supported the emperor and the imperial system. Three years later Yomiuri Newspaper surveyed public opinion about the emperor. At that time only 4% was negative to the imperial system. 87.5% favoured the emperor system in a survey conducted by the *Tokyo Newspaper* in 1975. These surveys reached beyond the student population.

When a typhoon is hitting us we must battle against it. Our wooden doors must be doubly secured, window latches engaged, and even the roofs must be reinforced. Japanese houses are not so strong. Once the typhoon is gone, we relax. Let's forget about it. This is Japanese *taifu-ikka* ('as soon as typhoon is gone . . . ') psychology. The Pacific War was a devastating typhoon. It raged murderously for fifteen years from 1931, when Japanese military activity began in Manchuria, to 1945 Hiroshima. But now . . . the typhoon is gone. Past is past. Let's not blame each other. Don't be 'unforgiving' and 'unforgetting'. There is a marked difference between the Japanese attitude towards the Far Eastern War Criminal Trial and the German attitude towards the Nürnberg War Trial. The former tend to 'forget' and 'forgive' while the latter repeatedly investigate the location of responsibility and the structure of the evil committed.

kichi   kyo

In this sense, the Japanese people are easy going in comparison with the German people. The Japanese people are basically optimistic. They believe in a happy-ending. In the ancient stratum of Shinto thought (*Ko-Shinto*) there are two cosmic principles; *kichi* (good, the Chinese character used here portrays the image of a mouth full of food) and *kyo* (evil, the Chinese character carries the image of a mouth empty of food). There are *kichi* gods and *kyo* gods. The *Ko-Shinto* affirms the ultimate superiority of the *kichi* gods over the *kyo* gods, good harvest over famine. The *kyo* principle is only as an agent to induce the higher *kichi*. The *kichi* uses the *kyo* to enhance itself. This dialectical outlook is already obvious in the *Kojiki* ('The Record of Ancient Matters') mythology. The primeval deities, Izanagi (male) and Izanami (female), procreate the universe. This is the work of *kichi*. But this *kichi* process of procreation, at its height, suddenly changes into *kyo*. Izanami gives birth to the fire-god, is burned to death and must go to the nether world. Izanagi, out of his affection for her, follows her to the underworld. Doing so he pollutes himself. This is the height of the *kyo*. But as soon as he comes out of the underworld, he washes himself in the clear stream and becomes clean again. Clean he becomes *kichi*. As he washes his left eye the sun goddess *Amaterasu* comes to be. This is the height of the *kichi* period. But the sun goddess is annoyed by the rude behaviour of *Susanoo*, the male god who is born when Izanagi washes his nose. She hides herself in the rock-cave. This is *kyo*. When the sun goddess steps out of the rock-cave the universe is full of light again. This is *kichi*.

The philosophy behind this is that *kyo* is not absolute. Always *kichi* prevails. *Kichi* is positive being. The end of the history is not *kyo*, but *kichi*. This is the view interpreted for us by the great Shinto scholar of eighteenth-century Japan, Motoori Norinaga.[18]

In this view of history as the alternating process of the *kichi* and the *kyo*, the mythological individual finds himself or herself in a certain momentum-process. The question of the moral responsibility of one's act is not to be pressed. As nature heals, the process (history) of the *kyo* turns to *kichi*. The 1945 experience of Hiroshima was the height of the *kyo*. But soon afterwards Japan was able to make a miraculous economic recovery leading to Expo 70. This is the *kichi*. The *kyo* may interrupt history. But *kichi* will prevail in the end. The Japanese people are *kichi*-optimists. Even Hiroshima was unable to change this Japanese metaphysics. The *taifu-ikka* psychology points in the same direction.

University students in Japan today live in a world quite different from the one leading up to 1945. Without inhibition they say what they think about the emperor and other political subjects. For them the war was something they hear about or read of in books. They have not seen Tokyo reduced to a wilderness and ruins by bombings. Any wisdom about history that the war generation may have got by going through painful experience must be transmitted to the younger generation. But this transmission is surrounded by many difficulties. One such difficulty is the persistence of Japanese *kichi*-optimism. All Japanese, young and old, share in this philosophy of life.

The Japanese people need to cultivate a more serious attitude towards history. In an obscure way, perhaps, the Japanese mind is now going through such a revolution. I cannot tell. It may be and it may be not. Is an ecological crisis pushing us to a more critically engaged relationship with history?

'Judge not, that you be not judged. For with the judgment you pronounce you will be judged, and the measure you give will be the measure you get . . . ' This passage does not suggest an easy-going life of *kichi*-optimism. 'Judge not!' not because of your optimism, but because of your realism! 'Judge not' does not mean 'do not take history seriously'. On the contrary, we must take history seriously to the extent that we realize our own blindness. How embarrassing!

The Japanese people will misunderstand this passage. They are tempted to think that 'judge not' means 'be easy with history' – for instance, the history of imperial absolutism, brutal execution of war in Asia and finally the utter destruction of the nation. Rather, 'Judge not . . . ' must mean 'Cultivate your faculty of discernment on what is happening in history. Take history seriously, as serious as you find "the log" in your own eye.'

To another he said, 'Follow me.' But he said, 'Lord, let me first go and
bury my father.' But he said to him, 'Leave the dead to bury their own
dead; but as for you, go and proclaim the kingdom of God.'

Luke 9.59,60

What is the kingdom of God if it is so important?

There are a number of parables on the theme of the kingdom of
God: The parable of the sower (Matt. 13.1–23; Mark 4.1–9; Luke
8.4–8); the parable of the weeds (Matt. 13.24–30); the parable of
the mustard seed (Matt. 13.31,32; Mark 4.30–32; Luke 13.18, 19);
the parable of the yeast (Matt. 13.33; Luke 13.20,21); the parable
of the hidden treasure (Matt. 13.44); the parable of the pearl (Matt.
13.45,46); the parable of the net (Matt. 13.47–50).

All these parables point to the presence of Jesus Christ whose
coming has brought a change in the world. He is the hidden centre
of the kingdom parables and all other parables. There are notes of
commitment, urgency, judgment, decision-making, wise-action, sur-
prise and the mystery of waiting found in these various images.
Man cannot be neutral and inactive in the presence of Jesus Christ.
He must think and act. In his study on the parables Joachim
Jeremias writes;

> The hour of fulfilment has come. . . . The strong man is disarmed,
> the powers of evil have to yield, the physician has come to the
> sick, the lepers are cleansed, the heavy burden of guilt is
> removed, the lost sheep is brought home, the door of the Father's
> house is opened, the poor and the beggars are summoned to the
> banquet, a master whose kindness is undeserved pays wages in
> full, a great joy fills all hearts. God's acceptable year has come.
> For there has appeared the one whose veiled majesty shines
> through every word and every parable – the Saviour.[19]

All these express the *Messianic Excitement*. Do we live in this
excitement? ' . . . he sells everything he has, and then goes back and
buys that field' . . . .

'Lord, let me first go and bury my father.' The father died and
must be buried. There is urgency. Jesus says that this urgency must
be interpreted in the light of the urgency of the kingdom of God.
Important as it is, the burial of the father must not be of supreme
importance. What a radical thing to say.

The great Jesuit missionary Francis Xavier came to Japan in

1549. The Jesuits were very perceptive of the culture of the country to which they came. In Japan they observed how important a funeral is. They made a special effort to show how meaningful the funeral is in the light of the Christian faith. A coffin is placed in the centre of the church with four huge candles lighted on the four corners surrounding it. Sermons were preached on the subject of Christian dying. The Jesuits gave equal importance to the funeral service of the rich and the poor. This impressed the Japanese people profoundly. On one such occasion, it is reported that more than 3000 people came to witness the funeral service of one poor man.

'Let the dead bury their own dead.' Francis Xavier was not dead, that is, not 'spiritually dead'. He was aflame with the messianic excitement. Living in the messianic excitement he was free and creative. He combined the funeral occasion with the proclamation of the messianic excitement. In this case 'the living' buried the dead. Life touched death. The messianic excitement excited the funeral procession. The urgency of the kingdom of God was communicated to the sixteenth-century Japanese.

When death and the messianic excitement are separated, then it happens that 'the dead bury their own dead'. The past is taking care of the past. What is happening does not have present and future meaning. 'Spiritually dead' means 'to live in the past'. The past is important. We are rooted in the past. Yet to live only in the past is negative and even deadening. The eighty years leading up to 1945 were demonic and destructive years for Japan. We must learn a lesson of history from those years. We must live that lesson in the context of today. We must make the past meaningful in the present so that we will have a future. The post war New Constitution of Japan which took effect on 3 May 1947 has this to say in the preamble:

> We, the Japanese people, . . . resolved that never again shall we be visited with the horrors of war through the action of government, do proclaim that sovereign power resides with the people and do firmly establish this Constitution. . . .

> We, the Japanese people, desire peace for all time and are deeply conscious of the high ideals controlling human relationship, and we have determined to preserve our security and existence, trusting in the justice and faith of the peace-loving peoples of the world. We desire to occupy an honoured place in an international society striving for the preservation of peace, and the banishment of tyranny and slavery, oppression and intolerance for all time from the earth. We recognize that all peoples of the world have the right to live in peace, free from fear and want.

We believe that no nation is responsible to itself alone, but that laws of political morality are universal; and that obedience to such law is incumbent upon all nations who would sustain their own sovereignty and justify their sovereign relationship with other nations.

We, the Japanese people, pledge our national honour to accomplish these high ideals and purposes with all our resources.

This preamble is very important. It expresses the sense of national repentance. It expresses the nation's desire to start a new life. In repentance Japan cannot allow the past to bury the past. It must be buried meaningfully and intelligently. It must be buried in the living engagement with the present. The past with all its ugliness must be examined in the light of the messianic excitement of Jesus Christ. In the messianic excitement is the future. 'We, the Japanese people, pledge our national honour to accomplish these high ideals and purposes with all resources.' In this resolution I see the violent past of Japan is brought captive to the mind of God in Jesus Christ.

30   Responsible King and Irresponsible King

> . . . they made kings, but not through me. They set up princes, but without my knowledge.   *Hosea 8.4*

In Israel God's kingship stands in a critical tension with the earthly human kingship. There always existed some circle within Israel to view the presence of human kingship as an apostasy since only God is the king. ' . . . they made kings, but not through me. They set up princes, but without my knowledge.' The human king must be placed under the divine king. The Egyptian, Sumerian, Babylonian and Hittite patterns do not have this dimension of a God as king judging the human king. But Hebrew king must know that he is only a *human* king. He must not become divine. When the human king becomes divine, he rules his people by fear-politics. The people are intimidated and threatened.

Moloch was a god foreign to Israel to whom human sacrifice was made in the midst of Israel. Israel had experience of both kinds of king:

'I am the Lord, your Holy One, the Creator of Israel, your King' (Isa. 43.15).

and the Moloch the one who makes one's children pass through the fire (Lev. 18.21; I Kings 11.7; Jer. 32.35).

The denunciation of the Moloch in the eyes of the people of the responsible king was focused on the abomination of the human sacrifice. The mark of Moloch is human sacrifice. In modern time the Auschwitz Hitler who made Anne Frank walk through the fire was a devouring Moloch. One of the most terrifying tales of the Valley of Hinnom is *The Gulag Archipelago* by Alexander Sol-zhenitsyn. Stalin was not an ordinary human. He was 'something more'.

Evidently evildoing also has a threshold magnitude. Yes, a human being hesitates and goes back and forth between good and evil all his life. He slips, falls back, clambers up, repents, things begin to darken again. But just so long as the threshold of evildoing is not crossed, the possibility of returning remains, and he himself is still within reach of our hope. But when, through the density of evil actions, the result either of their own extreme degree or of the absoluteness of his power, he suddenly crosses that threshold, he has left humanity behind, and without, perhaps, the possibility of return.[20]

The concept of Moloch and of absolute power go together.

The Moloch seeks human sacrifice. In 1937 Japan saw the pub-lication of *Kokutai no Hongi*, or Cardinal Principles of the National Entity of Japan. (In 1945 this book was prohibited by the Allied Occupation Force in the 'Directive for the Disestablishment of State Shinto'.) A few paragraphs point to the beatification of the Moloch ideology, the idea which finally ruined the nation:

Our country is established with the Emperor, who is a descen-dant of Amaterasu Ohmikami, as her center, and our ancestors as well as we ourselves constantly behold in the Emperor the fountainhead of her life and activities. . . . Hence, offering our lives for the sake of the Emperor does not mean so-called self-sacrifice, but the casting aside of our little selves to live under his august grace and the enhancing of the genuine life of the people of a State.

In our country, the two Augustnesses, Izanagi no Mikoto and Izanami no Mikoto, are ancestral deities of nature and the deities, and the Emperor is the divine offspring of the Imperial Ancestor who was born of the two Augustnesses. . . .

Bushido may be cited as showing an outstanding characteristic of our national morality. In the world of warriors one sees inherited the totalitarian structure and spirit of the ancient clans peculiar to our nation. Hence, though the teachings of Confucianism and Buddhism have been followed, these have been transcended. That is to say, though a sense of indebtedness binds master and servant, this has developed into a spirit of self-effacement and of meeting death with a perfect calmness.[21]

'The Imperial Way' (*Kōdō*) of Japan was a deceptive way. We lived in the disguised Moloch system until the bombing of Hiroshima in 1945. In following the Imperial Way 2526 young men perished between 25 October 1944 and 15 August 1945 on the suicide plane strategy named after the *kamikaze*, 'Divine Wind' which crashed the Mongolian invading fleets in the thirteenth century. The high ranking officers who planned this final desperate method manoeuvred to survive the war. The Moloch is deceptive and devouring.

In the critical year of 1941 there were four Imperial Conferences held on the issue of 'The Essentials for Carrying Out the Empire's Policies' vis-à-vis the attitudes of the United States, Great Britain and the Netherland. In all these four Imperial Conferences the emperor consistently remained silent, including the final one on 1 December 1941 which ratified the decision to make war. The prime minister Tojo Hideki was recorded to have concluded the Conference with the following remark:

> I would now like to make one final comment. At the moment our Empire stands at the threshold of glory or oblivion. We tremble with fear in the presence of His Majesty. We subjects are keenly aware of the great responsibility we must assume from this point on. Once His Majesty reaches a decision to commence hostilities, we will all strive to repay our obligations to him, bring the Government and the military ever closer together, resolve that the nation united will go on to victory, make an all-out effort to achieve our war aims, and set His Majesty's mind at ease. I now adjourn the meeting. During today's Conference, His Majesty nodded in agreement with the statements being made, and displayed no sign of uneasiness. He seemed to be in an excellent mood, and we were filled with awe.[22]

'We tremble with fear.' 'We were filled with awe.' Does any American say he trembles with fear in the presence of President Roosevelt? The emperor silently nods. He transcends science and democracy. He nods even though he knows that the petroleum reserve for the war operation will last only eighteen months. At the moment of grave decision making whether or not to take the nation into war, and to engulf all Asia into immense suffering, he remains 'absolutely' silent. The divine emperor in the Japanese manifestation was irresponsible to the world and to history at this moment. In three major wars Japan fought, against China (1894), against Russia (1904) and against United States, Great Britain and the Netherlands (1941) Japanese military actions occurred before the declaration of war. It seems to me that transcendental imperial divinity does not pay attention to the importance of human communication. The emperor stood outside the context of history. For a human being to stand above history 'with divine dignity' is pagan. It is irresponsibility called paganism. Irresponsible holiness is the characteristic of the Moloch holiness. The Moloch is irresponsible yet tries to be 'holy'. *Therefore* he must seek human sacrifice.

Holiness plus irresponsibility produces destruction.

The divine emperor was the head of the divine land. The Japanese soldiers were called *Shin Pei*, 'divine soldiers'. After the war we came to know the brutal and inhuman acts of our divine soldiers. Japan became all-divine and all-irresponsible. Japan grasped holiness for her own gain. This caused her destruction.

31   Invisible God and Visible Man

> All who make idols are nothing, and the things they delight in do not profit; their witnesses neither see nor know, that they may be put to shame.   *Isaiah 44.9*

The faith of Israel is against making God visible. A visible God is, in truth, not a God. It is an idol. Thus it stands opposed to one of the most fascinating preoccupations of man – making God visible! Even to make a crocodile or hornbill visible is quite an exciting enterprise, as we see from the work of the people of Kalimantan, Indonesia. Crocodile we know and hornbill we can see. But to recreate them by carving a piece of wood is to make them doubly visible. A crocodile in the muddy water is naturally visible. Carved and curved in wood it is 'religiously' visible. The naturally visible crocodile is not as interesting as a crocodile religiously visible. In the art form it is spiritualized. It has a spiritual message for man. It speaks our human language. It is heavily influenced by man. One may say it is 'anthropomorphized'. Such a crocodile is without a doubt much more interesting than a natural one. Indeed, many may even worship it.

The image of crocodile is carved by man. This image comes from the mind of man. The natural crocodile has been adjusted by the mind of man so that it will say what man wants it to say. The 'spiritual crocodile' is controlled by its creator. We might call it a theology of ventriloquism (*venter* the belly, *loqui* from *locutus*, to speak). The crocodile says what the carver wants it to say. This arrangement has high amusement value, because in ventriloquism the master can be carried away by his own enthusiasm. He may say something he might not have otherwise thought of! He may himself be surprised by what he sees in the carved crocodile! Yet, he must know that he himself has 'spiritualized' the crocodile.

Israel is against making God visible. Israel rejects the theology of ventriloquism. It knows that God made visible is a controlled God saying what man wants him to say. If man puts God into his scheme of ventriloquism he will imagine himself to be secure, enlarged, powerful. What a security to be in command of God!

The theology of ventriloquism is perhaps far more complicated than we think. The reason for this is that when we read the Bible we hear what we want to hear. We do not hear what we do not want to hear. In this sense the principle of ventriloquism is at work. Who among us is free from this temptation? . . . 'When the Spirit of truth comes, he will guide you into all the truth, . . . ' (John 16.13).

'All who make idols are nothing.' 'Nothing' in this context means 'chaos'. They are engaged in a chaotic enterprise. This chaotic pursuit has its own thrill. Man desires to enlarge himself with prestige, money, position, education, influence. . . . All things by which man expresses self-enlargement tend to become idols. Idol-atry is an enlargement of self (self-glorification) but it is not a deepening of self. In this way idols bring indignity to man. ' . . . their witnesses neither see nor know, that they may be put to shame.'

Man makes idols because he is lonely. 'When the people saw that Moses had not come down from the mountain but was staying there a long time, they gathered around Aaron and said to him "We do not know what has happened to this man Moses, who led us out of

Egypt; so make us a god to lead us" ' (Exod. 32.1). They are on a journey. Their leader is gone. They feel precarious. They feel lost. Make us a god to lead us. We often make idols because of our loneliness. Loneliness can be a moment of great spiritual creativity. Man who feels precarious is not lazy. He becomes alert. Yet, a misplaced sense of precariousness produces idolatry. We find quick remedy not in the deepening of self but in enlargement of self.

The true God is invisible. The true man is visible. Man, invisible, is a dangerous idol. For the first fifteen years of my life I lived in Japan ruled by the invisible emperor. He was thought to be too sacred to be seen by the common people. His face is referred to as the 'Dragon Face' meaning symbolically the most awesome and auspicious face. His voice is called 'Dragon Voice' or 'Diamond Voice'. In fact he was a god, not man, until 15 August 1945. Until then he was invisible. While he was invisible Japan engaged in the enforced emperor-worship cult. This history has made me suspicious of the invisible man.

In 1871 the Japanese Government, as it was pressed by the need to issue Japanese paper currency, made a study of the designs that appear on the currencies of other countries. They found that President Lincoln was on the American dollar (side face). Peter the Great appeared in the Imperial Russian currency (right side face, 1702). Napoleon was on the five franc silver coin (1804) and George III was on the six shilling coin (1804). However, the Japanese Government decided against using the image of the Emperor Meiji on its currency. The divine image of the emperor was thought to be too sacred to be used in this way. Instead, the image of a dragon, symbolic of the divine personality of the Emperor appeared on the currency. Whenever I see the image of Queen Elizabeth II on the New Zealand currency, I feel relaxed. She is visible. This symbolism is significant for the Japanese who is above forty-five years old today.

32   Midwives Who Feared God

> But the midwives feared God, and did not do as the king of Egypt commanded them, but let the male children live.   *Exodus 1.17*

'Then Joseph died, and all his brothers, and all that generation. But the descendants of Israel were fruitful and increased greatly. They multiplied and grew exceedingly strong; so that the land was filled with them' (Exod. 1.6,7). The Egyptians felt threatened by the increasingly powerful presence of the Hebrews. The king of Egypt commanded; 'when you serve as midwife to the Hebrew women, and see them upon the birthstool, if it is a son, you shall kill him; but if it is a daughter, she shall live' (1.16). The midwives disobeyed the command.

They feared God. They feared the invisible God. They feared the God who does not have chariots and army, fortress and palace, and political structure and economic supremacy. Against the visible presence of the king of Egypt, the midwives feared the invisible God. I am sure the midwives were afraid of the king of Egypt. But courageously they acted according to the higher principle of morality they knew. They knew that murdering the male babies at their birth as commanded is against the mind of God. They feared the king. But they feared God more. 'We must obey God rather than men' (Acts 5.29).

The king of Egypt was 'fearless' when he issued such a destructive command. A 'fearless' world, in this sense, is a dangerous world. Fearlessness can be the expression of complete secularism. The king of Egypt did not fear God. He was a 'secular' person in spite of all the rich religious symbolisms which surrounded him. How strange. The title Pharaoh means 'the great house'. It means the one who lives in the Great House. No house can be a great house without the touch of some kind of gods. At his coronation an Egyptian king received prenomen. The prenomen of Rameses II was User-maat-Re, 'Strong is the right of Ra.' It was believed that the kings came from the realm of the gods. They were god-kings. Ra was the solar god. It was the king, the god-king, who made the Great House great.

Yet the mid-wives feared God rather than this god-king. In every society we need 'midwives who fear God'.

This does not mean that we need 'religious people' or more religious organizations and systems. We need all kinds of people who 'fear God'. We need economists who fear God, politicians who fear God, educators who fear God, doctors who fear God. We need social midwives who fear God. They do not have to be 'religious'. They *fear God*. They stand against the power of the occupants of the Great House when they misuse their power. The midwives are ready to disobey the command. They may not be Christians, Muslims, Buddhists, or Jewish. They may call themselves 'secular' and 'non-religious'. . . . But they fear God.

'Secular' people, we think, do not fear God. 'Religious' people fear God. But is it really so? How do we draw the line between secular and religious people? If it is true that *only* religious people fear God why do we often see that religious people are more arrogant toward God than secular people? Arrogant? Yes, in trying to domesticate God to suit their own religious taste. Instead of fearing God, they use God to their self-enhancement. 'God, I thank thee that I am not like other men, extortioners, unjust, adulterers, or even like this tax collector. I fast twice a week, I give tithes of all that I get' (Luke 18.11,12). God is adjusted to man's religious taste. How often God is 'theologically' tamed! It often takes theology – what a tragedy – to adjust God to man's liking.

Are secular people free from this danger? No. They adjust God to their liking too. But they do not begin their adjustment programme with the introduction; 'God, I thank thee . . . '. Their programme is simpler than that of the religious people. The 'God' they adjust to their own liking is the God of their own making. The God they make is predictably quite subject to their adjustment.

In every society we need 'midwives who fear God'.

Professor Tadao Yanaihara (1893–1961), economist, sociologist, educator and evangelist, was a disciple of Mr Uchimura Kanzo, the founder of the no-church movement in Japan. Yanaihara was critical about the Japanese government's colonial policy in Formosa, Korea and Manchuria. In 1937 he was forced to resign his professorship at Tokyo University. He never stopped his studied criticism of the Japanese government for its flagrant brutality and oppression of the fellow Asian peoples. In particular he was critical about Japan's imperialistic policy in Manchuria. After he resigned from the university, he began to publish his own periodical *Kashin* or *Good News*. *Kashin* was only one of the Christian journals which was critical of the government, yet, it alone against all difficulties and harassments, continued its criticism all through the war years and into the post-war period.

The January 1940 issue of *Kashin* sharply attacked the brutality in Nanking. The army general Matsui who was responsible for the atrocity of Nanking was received by a 'so-called Christian meeting'

with a standing ovation in November 1939. Yanaihara referred to
this incident in this issue and accused the 'so-called Christians' for
not demanding words of apology from the general. In June 1940
issue of *Kashin* he speaks of General Itagaki, the Commander of
the Japanese Army in China, who said that Japan was helping to
make China independent and that Japan had no intention of imperial aggression against China. Yanaihara pointed out that this was
not true.[23] Professor Yanaihara's Kashin did not speak only about
'spiritual and religious' matters. It addressed itself clearly and
loudly to the events that were taking place in his day. He feared
God. He was fearless because he feared God. He was in the tradition
of the prophets of the Old Testament. After the war he was rein-
stated at Tokyo University. He became the president of the university for two terms, succeeding Dr Nambara Shigeru, also a disciple
of Uchimura Kanzo.

On Easter Sunday, 26 March 1967, The United Church of Christ
in Japan (Kyodan) issued its Confession on the Responsibility During World War II. Let me quote the last three paragraphs of the
Confession:

> The Church, as 'the light of the world' and as 'the salt of the
> earth', should not have aligned itself with the militaristic pur-
> poses of the government. Rather, on the basis of our love for her
> and by the standard of our Christian conscience, we should have
> more correctly criticized the policies of our motherland. How-
> ever, we made a statement at home and abroad in the name of
> the Kyodan that we approved of and supported the war, and we
> prayed for victory.
>
> Indeed, as our nation committed errors we, as a Church,
> sinned with her. We neglected to perform our mission as a
> 'watchman'. Now, with deep pain in our heart, we confess this
> sin, seeking the forgiveness of our Lord, and from the churches
> and our brothers and sisters of the world, and in particular of
> Asian countries, and from the people of our own country.
>
> More than 20 years have passed since the war, and we are
> filled with anxiety, for our motherland seems unable to decide
> the course that we should follow; we are concerned lest she move
> in an undesirable direction due to the many pressures of today's
> turbulent problems. At this moment, so that the Kyodan can
> correctly accomplish its mission in Japan and the world, we seek
> God's help and guidance. In this way we look forward to tomor-
> row with humble determination.

I am not going to document here how the Kyodan approved and
supported the war. The tragic chapter of the Christian church

becoming obedient to the Japanese religion of *Ra* is now documented in the important publication *Jinja Mondai to Kiristo Kyo* 'Shinto Problems and Christianity.'[24]

In 1978 a small book was published by Japan's most prestigious Iwanami Publishing House. The book is titled *Shūkyō Dan Atsu O Kataru* or War-time Repression of Religions. Four of its six chapters describe the brutal destruction carried out by the Japanese government against religious groups other than Christianity. The government decided to demolish them because they were openly critical of the state ideology. These four groups (*Omoto, Hitono-Michi, Shinkō-Bukkyō* and *Hon-Michi*) are quite different from the biblical faith. On the basis of their faith they criticized the behaviour and philosophy of the powerful government. One chapter of the book is devoted to the Holiness group of Christianity. Here is a report on the cross-examination of Rev. Sugeno:[25]

> According to the Old and New Testament, which I understand is the basis of the creed you believe, all people are sinners. Is this correct?
>
> Yes. All men are sinful.
>
> Do you imply then the emperor himself is a sinner?
>
> A humble subject I am . . . how should I dare to speak about the august emperor? I am, however, willing to answer the question. As long as the emperor is human, he cannot be free from being sinful.
>
> Then, the Bible says that the sinners cannot be saved apart from the redemption done by Jesus Christ on the cross, does this mean that the emperor needs the redemption by Jesus Christ?
>
> With due reverence to the emperor, I must repeat what I said before. I believe the emperor needs the redemption by Jesus Christ as long as he is human.

Rev. Sugeno feared God. He had a difficult life. He died in prison. When a human is elevated to the divine the storm comes. The majority of the people will not resist the storm. But some dare to resist. They will not 'do as the king of Egypt commanded them'.

33 Only Thirty-four Years from Hiroshima!

> They made kings, but not through me. They set up princes, but without
> my knowledge.
>
> *Hosea 8.4*

Hosea was one of the earliest of the prophets of Israel. Hosea's
ministry to the northern kingdom of which Samaria was the capital
followed closely upon that of Amos. Hosea lived through the unsettling time of the Assyrian threat. Finally Samaria fell to the Assy-
rians in 721 BC. It was in this context that Hosea made his critical
comment about kings. In Israel God's kingship stands in a critical
tension with earthly human kingship. There always existed within
Israel some who felt the human kingship to be an apostasy since
only God is king. The following story is told about the foundation
of the kingship in Israel.

> Then all the elders of Israel gathered together and came to
> Samuel at Ramah and said to him, ' . . . now appoint for us a
> king to govern us like all the nations'. But the thing displeased
> Samuel when they said, 'Give us a king to govern us.' And the
> Lord said to Samuel, 'Hearken to the voice of the people in all
> that they say to you; for they have not rejected you, but they
> have rejected me from being king over them . . . you shall sol-
> emnly warn them, and show them the ways of the king who shall
> reign over them.'
> So Samuel told all the words of the Lord to the people who
> were asking a king from him. He said, 'These will be the ways
> of the king who will reign over you: he will take your sons and
> appoint them to his chariots and to be his horsemen, and to run
> before his chariots; and he will appoint for himself commanders
> of thousands and commanders of fifties, and some to plough his
> ground and to reap his harvest, and to make his implements of
> war and the equipment of his chariots. He will take your daugh-
> ters to be perfumers and cooks and bakers. He will take the best
> of your fields and vineyards and olive orchards and give them to
> his servants. He will take the tenth of your grain and of your
> vineyards and give it to his officers and to his servants. He will
> take your menservants and maidservants, and the best of your
> cattle and your asses, and put them to his work. He will take the
> tenth of your flocks, and you shall be his slaves. And in that day
> you will cry out because of your king, whom you have chosen for

yourselves; but the Lord will not answer you in that day' (I Sam. 8.4–18).

The words of Samuel echo throughout the centuries of human political history. Israel saw a subtle relationship between 'the rejection of God' and 'the ways of the king'.

The subject of emperor worship (absolute human kingship) is an existential one for any Japanese person who is above forty years of age today. Japan was placed under the cult of emperor worship for the span of seventy years up to 1945. In the last twenty years the cult reached its frenzied destructive intensity.

The Japanese concept of 'God' is quite different from that of Israel. The eighteenth-century scholar Motoori Norinaga writes on the Japanese concept of 'God', *kami*.

> Speaking in general, however, it may be said that *kami* signifies, in the first place, the deities of heaven and earth that appear in the ancient records and also the spirits of the shrines where they are worshipped. It is hardly necessary to say that it includes human beings. It also includes such objects as birds, beasts, trees, plants, seas, mountains and so forth. In ancient usage, anything whatsoever which was outside the ordinary, which possessed superior power or which was awe-inspiring was called *kami*. . . . Evil and mysterious things, if they are extraordinary and dreadful, are called *kami*.[26]

In the ancient times the emperors were spoken of as 'visible gods' or 'god in the form of man' (*akitsu-kami*) as it is reported in the *Many-Ōshū* ('A Collection of Myriad Leaves', seventh and eighth century). But these expressions were free from any absolutistic political ideology. They were written in the cultural context of a diffused concept of gods. But the recent experience is radically different from that of the past. Out of the horizon of the relaxed pantheistic culture in which god is everywhere and everything can be god, came the ugly and destructive monster of the absolutism of human kingship. It was a new experience for the Japanese people. The Meiji Government launched a massive and aggressive campaign to establish the 'divinity' of the emperor. Two documents mark the decisive point in this process; they are The Constitution of the Empire of Japan (1889) and the Imperial Rescript on Education (1890). In *Kokutai no Hongi* or 'Cardinal Principles of the National Entity of Japan' (1937) it is declared that the Divine Emperor rules the Divine Land and People. His august glory shall reach the ends of the universe. On this fanatical ideological basis Japan went into the war against the United States, Great Britain and the Netherland in 1941. The 1941 Declaration of War begins and ends with mythical language; 'We, by the grace of Heaven, Emperor of Japan seated on the throne of a line unbroken for ages eternal, . . . Hallowed spirits of our imperial ancestors guarding us from above, ...'

The years between 1941 and 1945 were marked by brutal exploitation of the people and natural resources for the war aims. 'He will take your . . . . ' What Samuel said in ancient Israel came to be relentlessly true. More than ten million people lost their lives throughout Asia because of the war. The war time government used the mythology contained in the *Kojiki* ('Record of Ancient Matters' completed in 712). The myth speaks about the divine origin of the imperial household. The original text of *Kojiki* is given in ninety-six pages in the small paperback of Iwanami Publishing House in Tokyo. And perhaps ten pages of it supplied enough material to produce the demonic cult of emperor worship which ultimately cost more than ten million lives between 1930 and 1945. A million per page. How dangerous a violent use of a myth can be.

The cult of emperor worship was ended by the two atomic bombs blasted over the Japanese cities in August 1945. Japan was reduced to ashes.

Japan does not have the tradition of Mount Sinai. The idea of a holy and jealous God who is very much concerned about social justice is foreign to the Japanese people. According to the Japanese culture, 'gods' and man are continuous. And this continuity underlies a spirit of optimism among the people. Though history may judge them, they feel it will continue without much disruption, and will come to a happy end for the Japanese people. Yet it is undeniable that Japan has gone through a period of nightmare and destruction. The Preamble of The Constitution of Japan (1947) expresses her determination not to repeat the tragedy of war again; 'We, the Japanese people, . . . resolved that never again shall we be visited with the horrors of war through the action of government, ...'

On 10 November 1976, the Japanese government sponsored the National Celebration for the Fiftieth Year of the Imperial Reign. Seven thousand, five hundred people gathered in Budo-Kan in Tokyo. The prime minister Takeo Miki led the thrice *Banzai*. This celebration was held under the tightest security precautions, and a nation divided watched it. In fact, the present emperor was enthroned in 1928. The fiftieth year of his reign falls in 1978. Yet, for political reasons, the government initiated this event. The date, 10 November, has a special meaning. It was on this date in 1940 that Japan celebrated her two thousand, six hundredth year of the founding of the nation. Since then this date has symbolized the rightist and fascist ideology.

In 1949 the United States changed its policy towards Japan because of the emergence of the People's Republic of China. Communist China posed a threat to Japan and the United States. Against this threat Japan must be 'strengthened'. From that time Japan began to revert to the pre-war imperial cult. I am not saying that the United States is wholly responsible for this fateful trend. The Japanese people gradually began to shout again 'Give us a king to govern us'. The same kind of king as they had before Hiroshima. After they have gone through all the traumatic experiences of 'the ways of the king'. There has been, unfortunately, every indication that the emperor is happy to play his fateful role in the coming back of state shintoism.

In April 1952 the emperor and the empress worshipped at Yasukuni Shrine, the shrine of the war-dead which had been the centre of war-time fascism and militarism. In 1953, with the budget of two billion yen raised voluntarily among the people, the Ise Grand Shinto Shrine was replaced by a new structure according to the tradition which goes back to the ancient time. In October 1958, the Meiji Shrine, which had been destroyed by air raids, was rebuilt. The shrine had been the enormous monument to emperor absolutism up to 1945. The Emperor and the Empress worshipped the Spirit of the Meiji emperor there in November of the same year. Since January 1959, the Japanese government (Liberal Democratic Party) has been working towards the nationalization of the Ise Grand Shinto Shrine. December 1966 saw the return of the Founding Nation Day, 11 February, the date which had been the symbol for the cult of the emperor worship for seventy years up to 1945. In 1974 the sixtieth replacement of the shrine by a new structure took place at Ise Grand Shinto Shrine. The Emperor and the Empress engaged in the act of religious worship there. On 15 August 1978, the Prime Minister Takeo Fukuda officially paid respect to the spirits of the war-dead. The nationalization of the Yasukuni Shrine has been one of the most important agendas for the government since 1969. Such a move is obviously contradictory to the provisions of the post-war Constitution of Japan.

Japan uses an Imperial Calendar. The year of the enthronement of the emperor is the first year of a new calendar. This is to show that time itself is a property of the imperial personage. This system of calendaring is called the *Gengo* system. AD 1978 corresponds to the fifty-third year of the present emperor. There is a strong rightist push to make the *Gengo* system an official law of the land. This move is a part of the total nationalistic movement towards the pre-war type of imperial system. The United Church of Christ in Japan (*Kyodan*) issued a statement opposing the Gengo Legislation in

September 1978:

According to reliable reports, there will be concerted efforts to pass the 'Gengo Legislation' at the next session of the Japanese Diet making the Imperial calendar an official law of the land. There have already been cases in regional legislatures of pushing through this legislation without any substantial discussion of the issues involved. Such procedures which expose the hidden intention of forcing through the 'Gengo Legislation' at this time cannot be separated from the various movements to 'Nationalize the Yasukuni Shrine', 'Revive the Imperial Rescript on Education', and 'Establish "Kimi ga yo" as the National Anthem', which are all in conjunction with the efforts to restore the 'Daijosai' (Shinto ceremony of thanksgiving in which the Emperor functions as a divinity), following the forthcoming accession of the new Emperor.

The steps being taken one after the other by the government to restore the various pre-war practices and systems which lost their legal basis under the present constitution of Japan, are not only in violation of the spirit of democracy, peace and human rights contained in the Constitution, but are a concerted effort to spur the reassertion of an ultra-nationalistic ideology.

For these above reasons, we herein express our strong opposition to the 'Gengo Legislation'.

Why is Japan running backwards so fast? Do we want Hiroshima again? All of these things, including a 2.1 trillion yen military budget for the Self-Defence-Force for the year starting 1979, are happening today.

Only thirty-four years from Hiroshima. 'He will take your sons
. . . .'

34   Uchimura Kanzo

For where two or three are gathered in my name, there am I in the midst of them.
                                                                    Matthew 18.20

One of the important names in the last hundred years of Christianity in Japan is Uchimura Kanzo (1861–1930). He was an independent evangelist, religious thinker, writer, critic and the founder of the *Mukyōkai* (no-church movement). The latest edition of his complete works, comprising 50 volumes (exegetical 17 volumes, theological and topical 25 volumes and correspondence and diaries 8 volumes) has been published by Kyōbunkan in Tokyo between 1961–1966. Uchimura is one of the most well read among the Christian writers of Japan. With his first book *Kiristo Shinto No Nagusame* or Divine Comfort Christians Experience (1893) he established himself as a Christian writer. Soon after publication, this book became a classic in Japanese Christian circles.

Uchimura's encounter with Christianity took place at Agricultural College in Sapporo, Hokkaido when he was seventeen years old. He came, with his friends, under the influence of William S. Clark, the president of the Massachusetts Agricultural College who was visiting for a brief period of six months at the invitation of the Japanese government. After much resistance the young Uchimura signed the document prepared by Clark, 'Covenant of Believers in Jesus'. Soon afterwards he was baptized by a Methodist missionary. From the day he signed it to the last day of his life he was faithful to the covenant and dedicated himself to the preaching of the gospel.

He studied theology for only half a year at Hartford Theological College in the United States. His original field of study was fishery. He loved the world of nature. His writings refer often to his study of the natural world.

The Constitution of the Empire of Japan was promulgated in 1889. The Imperial Rescript on Education was given to the people in 1890. The absolutism of the imperial system was fast becoming a powerful and ominous reality in Japan. In January 1891 there was a solemn ceremony of Receiving the Imperial Rescript on Education at the school where Uchimura was a member of the faculty. In this ceremony Uchimura refused to 'bow deeply in worship' to the Rescript. There were ninety teachers and more than a thousand students who watched Uchimura's 'impious' action. For the pantheistic Japanese 'worship' has never been a problem. Anything can be worshipped. Why not? Is not all 'divine' *kami*? This attitude of Uchimura was a new experience for the Japanese people. He took – very courageously indeed – the issue of 'worshipping' seriously. His theology did not allow him to worship the Rescript. The tradition of Mount Sinai entered the land of Mount Fuji at this moment. One must not worship the Rescript. Only worship God. He was called an 'enemy of the nation'. He resigned his position. Out of this painful experience came his first book.

The complete text of the Imperial Rescript on Education is as follows:

Know ye, Our subjects:
Our Imperial Ancestors have founded Our Empire on a basis broad and everlasting, and have deeply and firmly implanted virtue; Our subjects ever united in loyalty and filial piety have from generation to generation illustrated the beauty thereof. This is the glory of the fundamental character of Our Empire, and herein also lies the source of Our education. Ye, Our subjects, be filial to your parents, affectionate to your brothers and sisters; as husbands and wives be harmonious, as friends true; bear yourselves in modesty and moderation; extend your benevolence to all; pursue learning and cultivate arts, and thereby develop intellectual faculties and perfect moral powers; furthermore, advance public good and promote common interests; always respect the Constitution and observe the laws; should emergency arise, offer yourselves courageously to the State; and thus guard and maintain the prosperity of Our Imperial Throne coeval with heaven and earth. So shall ye not only be Our good and faithful subjects, but render illustrious the best traditions of your forefathers.

The Way here set forth is indeed the teaching bequeathed by Our Imperial Ancestors, to be observed alike by Their Descendants and the subjects, infallible for all ages and true in all places. It is Our wish to lay it to heart in all reverence, in common with you, Our subjects, that we may all attain the same virtue.

Uchimura made a delicate distinction. He said the Rescript must be practised but not worshipped.

What is *Mukyōkai*? *Mu* means 'nothing' and *kyōkai*, church. Hence *Mukyōkai* is often translated as 'no-church movement'. Uchimura writes: '*Mukyōkai* is a church for those who have no church. It is like a dormitory for those who have no home. It is a spiritual home of protection or orphanage. *Mu* of *Mukyōkai* means "(those who) do not have". It does not mean "to reduce to nothing" or "to ignore".' To Uchimura the churches seemed so concerned about their systems and organizations that they had lost the dimension of spiritual freedom and vitality. They had become organizations instead of the household of God. He held that while life takes form and system, it is at the same time free from them. Life comes first and system second. Isaiah and Jeremiah and other prophets were, according to Uchimura, people of *Mukyōkai* movement.

The *Mukyōkai* meeting is centred upon the study of the Bible and prayer. There are no ministers, church buildings, no sacraments (baptism and eucharist). Uchimura conducted Bible study groups throughout Japan and published his periodical 'Study of the Bible' continuously all throughout his independent ministry. The last issue, Number 357, came out a month before his death. Uchimura's faith was neither rigid, legalistic nor indiscriminately inclusive. In all he proclaimed the name of Jesus Christ. He did so fearlessly and most relevantly for his time. He was a keen observer of what was going on in the society of Japan at that time.

It is remarkable that in him we see a living and dynamic unity of spiritual concern and social concern. He was a most dedicated preacher of the sinfulness of man and of grace in the justification by faith. Yet at the same time, he was one of the foremost critics of social injustice and was himself much involved in the struggle against social ills. He was outspoken in his criticism of Japan's war against Russia. The unity between the spiritual concern and social concern came to him without effort. This is what made him so fascinating and compelling to his audience, the Japanese people. Often I wonder if the secret of this unity comes from his concentration on the message of Jesus Christ and his freedom from the organizational concerns – what he calls 'church-system'. He firmly believed the simple promise of Jesus: 'For where two or three are gathered in my name, there am I in the midst of them.'

35 Peace in Time and Beyond Time

He said, 'Go into the city to such a one, and say to him, "The Teacher says, My time is at hand; I will keep the passover at your house with my disciples."' And the disciples did as Jesus had directed them, and they prepared the passover.   *Matthew 26.18,19*

The Buddha was often invited by his devotees to dinner. It is said that if the dinner arrangement was acceptable in terms of the rules of the community of the Buddha (*Sangha*) he accepted the invitation. But he accepted *in silence* without indicating any agreement or promise. He did not say: 'Thank you for your hospitality. I will be there. . . . ' Have we ever invited someone who accepted our dinner invitation in silence? We would not know how many pieces of chicken to fry! The Buddha wanted to be free from the grip of time. If promised that he would be at a certain place at a certain time, he would be less free. He appreciated the hospitality, but he saw the danger that time may get control over his inner freedom. He did not reject the invitation. He accepted it without uttering a word. He battled against the grip of time by the power of his inner freedom. That freedom expressed itself 'in silence'.

We believe in making appointments. Our life is made up of continuous appointments – perpetual 'I must be there at a certain time'. Important people have secretaries to keep their busy schedule of appointments flowing without mistakes. They are 'booked-up'. Booked-up people are successful people. He who has an appointment every fifteen minutes is more successful and important than he who has an appointment every half an hour. The Buddha sees differently. He wants to be above time and not subject to time. Of course, he lived in a different world from this world of ours. Yet he poses a meaningful question to us today. For the Buddha an appointment book is a symbol of slavery to time. Often I think of the Buddha accepting the dinner invitation in silence. I am fascinated by it. I have not dared to imitate him as yet.

It was 25 May 1945. All night Tokyo was bombed by the American B29s. Our tiny wooden house was reduced to ashes together with the whole of Tokyo. The morning came as though nothing had happened. I knew the morning came because I saw the sun rising over the devastated wilderness that had been Tokyo. I saw the sun, . . . but it was a sun I did not know. The sun I knew did not come up *that* morning. It was a different, strange sun that came up over the wilderness. Overnight Tokyo was changed. I felt homeless. I felt misplaced and lost. I felt an intolerable loneliness encircling me. Tokyo was a forsaken city and I a forsaken person. I was orphaned. I felt as though I had been deserted by time. . . . as though submerged into lifeless timelessness.

For eighty busy 'booked-up' years up to 1945 Japanese history was irreverent towards the dignity of man. It was demonic and destructive. But all the while we had been very busy. We paid least attention to the inner freedom in which is the dignity of man. The eighty 'booked-up' years of fanatic expansionism and militarism of Japan suddenly came to end by the two atomic bombs in August 1945. Since the war Japan has been 'booked-up' again by its own determination to pursue economic strength. She has not been lazy. This is good. 'If any one will not work, let him not eat' (II Thess. 3.10). On 23 August 1978, the Japanese Government disclosed that the proposed budget for Japan Self Defence Force in the year 1979 reaches the staggering sum of 2.1 trillion yen. It ranks the seventh in the whole world. This point we have reached thirty-four years after Hiroshima. We have been busy reconstructing the nation. Yes, but . . . something must have gone decisively wrong in the mean-time. I do not want to experience 25 May 1945 again.

Can't we have a good healthy life without returning to militarism? Is this an idiotic dream? Or is it a possibility in the world today? Why can't we be booked-up in things that will give mankind peace and harmony?

The disciples of Jesus prepare the passover. They do as Jesus directs them. Jesus books the meeting for himself and for his disciples. Why? It is neither his birthday party nor a political propaganda party. The reason is given in the shortest sentence: 'My time is at hand'. The Greek New Testament word for *time* here is *kairos*. In contrast to *chronos* (clock time, 'chronology') the word *kairos* points to the qualitative element of the occasion, the decisive moment. Jesus says that his decisive moment is at hand. The passover observance points to the secret of this decisive moment. The time of his suffering is at hand. In his freedom he faces this critical time. He directs his disciples to get ready for this time which is to shake all clock time. It is the time prepared by God himself. Within that time the disciples prepare the passover meal.

The ministry of Jesus is now focused on this critical moment. It is not a moment of silence but of the proclamation of the Word of God. Through the whole of his personality and life he takes up the task of proclamation. . . . That is, he proclaims the love of God through his suffering for man. He decisively wants to have this occasion of passover meal with his disciples. This important booking is crucial in the experience of mankind. When he says 'My time is at hand', *chronos* is shaken by the *kairos*.

On 25 May 1945, I felt as though chronological time had come to a full stop. I felt as though I was swallowed up by an uncanny and meaningless timelessness. I felt so threatened. When Jesus said 'my time is at hand', the ordinary chronological time also stopped. It was deeply disturbed. But when *chronos* stopped the new time of salvation, instead of a time of meaninglessness, came. Apart from this *kairos* of Jesus Christ, our busy booked-up life will most likely produce again and again a kind of world which makes every nation to budget enormous sums for military hardware.

The Buddha directs our attention to the peace *beyond* time. Jesus Christ invites us to experience peace *in* time. The former values timelessness, the latter timefulness. Time is filled when the act of love fills it up. This 'fullness of time', this love which makes time meaningful – this opposes the 2.1 trillion yen military budget of Japan.

IV Justice Insisting

36 The Good Samaritan Today

But he, desiring to justify himself, said to Jesus, 'And who is my neighbour?' Jesus replied, 'A man was going down from Jerusalem to Jericho, and he fell among robbers, who stripped him and beat him, and departed, leaving him half dead. Now by chance a priest was going down that road; and when he saw him he passed by on the other side. So likewise a Levite, when he came to the place and saw him, passed by on the other side. But a Samaritan, as he journeyed, came to where he was; and when he saw him, he had compassion, and went to him and bound up his wounds, pouring on oil and wine; then he set him on his own beast and brought him to an inn, and took care of him. And the next day he took out two denarii and gave them to the innkeeper, saying, "Take care of him; and whatever more you spend, I will repay you when I come back." Which of these three, do you think, proved neighbour to the man who fell among the robbers?' He said, 'The one who showed mercy on him.' And Jesus said to him, 'Go and do likewise.'   *Luke 10.29–37*

I

The biblical God suffers at the disruption of peace in the human community. Where is the man who is fallen among robbers? . . . 'Where is Abel your brother?' (Gen. 4.9). 'Can a woman forget her sucking child that she should have no compassion on the son of her womb? Even these may forget, yet I will not forget you' (Isa. 49.15).

We live outside of Eden. Outside of Eden injury takes place. Injury may be healed and wholeness (*shalom*) restored by someone's becoming a neighbour to the injured one. But *shalom* does not just happen. It requires doing from us.

Archbishop Dom Helder Camara initiated the Movement for Basic Education in Brazil in the early 60s. The text-book of the movement, *To Live is to Struggle*, has the following sentences:

Pedro's family is hungry. The people work and are hungry. Is it just that Pedro's family should be hungry? Is it just that the people are hungry? The people of Brazil are exploited. They are exploited not only by Brazilians but by many foreigners. How can we rescue the country from this condition?[27]

The American black theologian James Cone bitterly writes:

> . . . men dying of hunger, children maimed from rat bites, women
> dying of despair – and the Church passes a resolution.[28]

Shalom requires our active participation. The gospel demands us
to give up 'other-side-life-style'. Yet we pass by on the other side
quickly. Some of us slowly. Some of us without feeling guilty. Some
of us feeling guilty. Some of us confusedly and some of us timidly.
But we pass by.

'There was no place for them in the inn . . . . ' This is what Luke
tells us about the 'silent night and holy night' at Christmas. There
are 650,000 Koreans living today in Japan. They pay tax but they
have no votes. They live all their life in Japan yet they have no
citizenship. They are ignored, discriminated against and denied all
security and many other social benefits. There is no place for them
in Japan . . . . We pass by.

The Treaty of Waitangi was signed between the Maoris and the
white Settlers in 1840 in which 'sovereignty' over New Zealand was
transferred to Queen Victoria. Their land – that is their life – was
confiscated from them. They became strangers in their own land.
'. . . there was no place for them in their own inn'. . . . We pass by.
A twenty-seven year old man living in a hamlet outside a village in
Tamil Nadu told an interviewer in 1971:

> We cannot go to the village post office, because it is in Brahmin
> Street. And that street is barred to the Harijans. If we need
> postage stamps or stamped envelopes, we have to ask a Mudliar
> or Naiker (local low-caste Hindus) to get them for us. We dare
> not try to go to the Post Office. If we did, all the caste Hindus
> will join together, and beat us.

> Won't the police contingent posted in the village protect you?

> No, they are all caste Hindus, except one. And that policeman
> looks the other way whenever he sees us. He likes to show that
> he is quite different from us. Anyway, there are other ways of
> punishing us: If we tried to act above our place in society, the
> village *karnam* (land revenue official) would refuse to put his
> signature on our papers. And we need that for any and every
> transaction made.[29]

. . . . We look the other way.

The Samaritan stops. He puts the man on his own animal and
takes him to an inn. He is willing to meet the lodging and medical
expense. He is able to do so because he has his own money. The
parable does not say that he robbed others and paid the expense.

He makes his money by honest work, I would imagine. He does not give up everything for the man in need. What he does is not dramatic. He does a reasonable thing. With compassion he takes care of him. The parable is realistic. In this un-dramatic way *shalom* returns to the community. There are many grades of Samaritans possible. But the essential qualification is to become a neighbour to the needy. 'Blessed are the merciful, for they shall obtain mercy' (Matt. 5.7). All grades of Samaritans can participate in the call made by Archbishop Camara and the black theologian Cone.

Mother Teresa of Calcutta stops. She does what she can do. She does not suffer from any self-importance complex. Only by-standers think that what Mother Teresa is doing is dramatic. She does not. Love expresses itself through discipline. Love expressing itself in dramatic and sensational ways is cheap love. 'We are unworthy servants; we have only done what was our duty' (Luke 17.10).

II

The fundamental life philosophy of the Japanese people is 'continuity'. If something continues it is felt to be prosperous. The line of imperial succession is continuous. Everything possible will be done to ensure that the family name will be continued. Production and sales must be continued. When continuity is disrupted disintegration sets in. The 'next-next' eternally continuing line is the prosperous line. There is no beginning and no end. Only 'next-next' is.[30]

This is a busy philosophy. The 'next-next' will naturally pick up momentum. This is very much welcomed. The momentum carries man along with it until he finds himself submerged in the 'next-next process'. No one has time to look around and pay attention to others. All are submerged in the same 'next-next process'.

I find this 'next-next' philosophy becoming the characteristic of all the technologically developed industrial countries. The 'next-next' view of life has something deeply satisfying and attractive to our mind. Who likes discontinuity? Who wants the end to come? What indeed is prosperity if it is not continuity?

The basic Japanese life philosophy, then, is not congruous to the mind of the Good Samaritan, whose *next* travel schedule is disrupted by the victim he unexpectedly meets on the way. The Good Samaritan has no time for the next until this human need of his neighbour is met.

The fundamental life philosophy of the Thai people is 'retribution'; 'if you do wrong you will harvest evil, if you do good you will be blessed with good'. This principle of retribution, which is called *karma*, answers all kinds of difficult questions about life for which no proper explanation can be found. 'It must be the *karma* that this happened to him. . . .' The victim on the way to Jericho, in the parable of Jesus, is fallen by his own *karma*. It was not an accident but an elaborate system of retribution working itself out on the man. Such a view of life, has a negative influence upon social action. Individually or collectively, we are what we are – poor, hungry, oppressed, sick – because of the *karma*. It is our own fault. It is inevitable.

Again, I find something similar to this Thai view of life evident outside of Thailand. In the Western industrial technological society we live more or less by the principle: 'You make your own money. And you make your own life.' What you are is known in terms of the money you make. The *karma* attitude is appreciated among people who are doing well because it can teach people who are not doing well to accept their lot. Somehow, it is their own fault that they have not done well.

The Good Samaritan rejects the spirit of both the Japanese 'next-next' and the Thai *karma*. He allows his programme to be disrupted. He does not look at the victim through the doctrine of *karma*, but with compassion; 'when he saw him, he had compassion. . . .' This was the man who acted as neighbour to the man in need.

III

The Good Samaritan made certain arrangements for the recovery of the victim. He 'went to him and bound up his wounds, pouring on oil and wine' (first aid operation – emergency care), 'he set him on his own beast' (ambulance service), 'and brought him to an inn' (hospitalization), 'next day he took out two denarii and gave them to the innkeeper' (medical expense). . . . Such action, directed to the restoration of wholeness to man, is in the genuine and healthy sense 'political'. What else can be the goal of all human political actions other than the restoration of wholeness to the human community? The whole parable is concentrated in the political subject; 'Who is my neighbour?'

I would like to quote from 'Prayer of Life' by Sudhakar S. Ramteke, Director of Durgapur Industrial Service in India:

. . . . I am old now.
They say I am going to die soon.
What a relief.
They tell me that I should go to the mission hospital, and consult

a doctor. The doctor examines me and he says I have to take X-Ray, injections and may be operation.
I say Doctor, How can I finance this?
He says, that is your problem, my hospital must become self-supporting.
I went to a government hospital, after several visits they examined me and gave me several prescriptions, but only one red medicine all the time free of costs.
No relief so far.
Whether I survive or not, is not important any way.

I was thinking what is next.
Thou need not worry about me my Lord. I have tremendous capacity to suffer.

They tell me that I am bound to go to hell (if there is any) because I was a sinner and a criminal throughout my life.
But as I have tremendous capacity to suffer, may be Thy hell (if there is any) and judgement, I believe will be more humane and comforting than the hell and judgement on this earth created by Thy people.

I couldn't have done better than this.
We anxiously wait for Thy Kingdom to come on this earth.
My last prayer to Thee O Lord, inspire, motivate and convince Thy Govt., Thy Society, Thy Church, Thy good people, so that they can
'Love Thy neighbour' in concrete terms by actions.
So they struggle with us in our suffering and struggle,
and find hope in our hope i.e., Thy hope.
It is high time my Lord.
I have finished my Lord.
I am ready for your mercy or for your judgement.

Amen.[31]

Here is a man in need. He needs ambulance service, hospitalization and medical insurance. All passed by him. He accepted this painful fact. What else can he do? 'Thou need not worry about me my Lord. I have tremendous capacity to suffer!' he says. Is this the voice of despair or of cynicism? One thing is clear, that the destructive force of 'all passing by' has made this man despaired and resigned. Good politics must fight against the 'all passing by'. The primary attention of politics must be directed to the weaker members of the community. This is precisely the spirit of God's politics.

When you make your neighbour a loan of any sort, you shall not go into his house to fetch his pledge.

. . . . And if he is a poor man, you shall not sleep in his pledge; when the sun goes down, you shall restore to him the pledge that he may sleep in his cloak and bless you; and it shall be righteousness to you before the Lord your God. . . . You shall give him his hire on the day he earns it, before the sun goes down (for he is poor, and sets his heart upon it); lest he cry against you to the Lord, and it be sin in you. . . . You shall not pervert the justice due to the sojourner or to the fatherless, or take a widow's garment in pledge; but you shall remember that you were a slave in Egypt and the Lord your God redeemed you from there; therefore I command you to do this (Deut. 24.10–18).

In 1935 Reinhold Niebuhr was invited to Pineville, Kentucky. Niebuhr found himself in the midst of conflict between the poor miners and the middle class mining operators and owners. The middle class churches stood on the side of the middle class mining operators and owners. Clergy became vocal in saying that they are against 'communists' and 'union organizers'. There in the small town he observed 'religion' functioning as the bastion of social conservatism, preventing 'a thorough analysis of the human problem' and resisting any alteration of the *status quo*. One operator was quoted as saying:

I am a good Christian and a member of the Christian Church, but I would just as soon tie a communist in a sack and throw him in the river as do anything else I know.

Town leaders considered themselves justifiably moral because they sponsored a charity program for some of the miners and because several weeks before the committee's arrival, a religious revival had brought 'salvation' to most of the individuals in the middle-class community.[32]

The oppressed want justice not charity. The rich want to give charity not justice. In particular, the powerful members of the community want to give 'religion' to the poor. 'Religion' will take away the complaints from the poor. It will teach them to expect their happiness in the 'beyond', the eternal bliss. The Pineville churches 'walked by on the other side' just as many other churches do. They did not stop. There is no Christian social ethics unless we stop as the Samaritan stopped.

'Ambulance service', 'hospitalization', 'medical insurance' and so on must be established in the community not as charity but as expressions of social justice. Those who can make their voices heard will get satisfaction from the state. But God's politics must hear the unuttered cry of one fallen and unable to cry.

IV

Let me quote from *Christian Conference of Asia News* (15 June, 1978)

On 1 March 1976, P. Rajan, a young engineering student in a city in the south of India, disappeared mysteriously from the college where he was studying. It was rumoured that he was taken away by the police. Only Rajan's aged father, a retired teacher, dared to make enquiries. The government denied that Rajan was ever arrested. Rajan's mother lost her mind.

Months later, after freedom was restored in India, it came to light that Rajan had been tortured by the police, and that he had died the very day that he was arrested. The Rajan case became big news. It had serious repercussions. In its wake the Chief Minister of the State had to submit his resignation. It led to the startling discovery that there were many similar disappearances and that torture was part of normal police work during the Emergency. . . .

One may be equally sure that Jessica Sales and Teotimo Tantiado, both of the Philippines . . . were not tortured or done to death by President Marcos. He has other and far more important things to think of – like the establishment of an Asian Regional Commission to look into alleged human rights violations and of a system of international inspections of prisons on a voluntary basis.

What happens to the Rajans and Jessicas of Asia, however, cannot be understood in isolation from the political trends and the moral continuum of human affairs in Asian nations. Authoritarianism breeds authoritarianism, and the further down the line the process penetrates, the more arbitrary, unimaginative and callous it becomes. It uses slaves to enslave people and, in the process, it brutalises beyond recognition those who run its errands.

For a long time it was fashionable in Asia to speak about the white domination which brutalized the Asians. Since 1950 this theme has rapidly become anachronistic. What we see today is that Asians are persecuting and murdering fellow Asians: Indians against Indians, Koreans against Koreans, Filipinos against Filipinos, and Cambodians against Cambodians. . . . The reality of Asians victimizing Asians has replaced the image of white exploitation and brutality. What we see today forces us to review our self-identity. History today is demonstrating to the whole world that Asian brutality against fellow Asians can be of extreme intensity.

Asians can no longer hold a simplistic self-image of 'innocent victim'. Human history is far more complex and treacherous than we were accustomed to think. What is happening in Asia is seen as well in many places in the world.

The Good Samaritan takes care of the victim who was left half dead. He takes reasonable steps for the recovery of the victim. In the human community the powerful are always beating up the weak. Victims are continually produced. We must seek to change the system that produces so many victims. The Good Samaritan of today must be concerned with the change of the social systems. He must be interested in prevention of exploitation and victimization, and not just in taking care of victims left half dead. The serious issue in front of the followers of the Good Samaritan today is; how to redistribute power in the community so that the powerful are checked in their blatant exploitation of the weak. This is the gigantic issue for the entire human community as well.

The Good Samaritan must be active in the area of prevention. Unless we can prevent evil from becoming unchecked 'authoritarianism will breed authoritarianism . . .' and many nameless people will suffer.

37   A 36 Billion Yen Temple

The Jews then said, 'It has taken forty-six years to build this temple, and will you raise it up in three days?' But he spoke of the temple of his body. When therefore he was raised from the dead, his disciples remembered that he had said this; and they believed the scripture and the word which Jesus had spoken.   *John 2.20–22*

Our life style today is strictly outlined by the power of hard-cash. Why could it not be outlined instead by the wealth of human-relationship?

We want to live a resourceful and abundant life. But we are constantly instructed that a resourceful and abundant life will be expensive. If it costs a lot it will be good. Going to Hawaii for a vacation is a good idea since it is expensive. This car is good because it costs a lot. Only expensive restaurants are really good places to eat. I cannot deny that there is some truth in all this. Good food, good living environment, good education, good medical care, good transportation cost a lot. They do contribute a great deal to our quality of life. But might it not be a possibility that there is a less expensive, more resourceful life style? Our civilization has equated expensiveness with resourcefulness. Is this a valid equation? In 1970 the sociologist Philip Slater wrote thus of American life:

> We seek a private house, a private means of transportation, a private garden, a private laundry, self-service stores, and do-it-yourself skills of every kind. An enormous technology seems to have set itself the task of making it unnecessary for one human being ever to ask anything of another in the course of going about his daily business. Even within the family Americans are unique in their feeling that each member should have a separate room, and even a separate telephone, television, and car, when economically possible. We seek more and more privacy, and feel more and more alienated and lonely when we get it.[33]

Our technological resourcefulness is making our life expensive and lonely. Technology is ambiguous. It can enrich and impoverish our life. Technology is like fire; it can cook rice for our enjoyment and nutrition and it can also reduce our house to ashes.

Can we bring about an inexpensive yet resourceful life style? One way – perhaps the only way – to do this would be to cultivate, increase and deepen human relationship. Human relationship is inexpensive yet resourceful. This is grace indeed. The biblical God is the God of a covenant relationship with man. This means that the whole biblical teaching is rooted in *relationship*. Money has ultimate meaning only if it enhances human relationship. The salvation the Bible is talking about is 'inexpensive yet resourceful'. If salvation is expensive in terms of hard-cash, then something is wrong with that kind of salvation.

For the last twenty years we have witnessed a boom of spectacular religious buildings in Japan. 'New religions' are competing with each other in the size and grandeur of such building projects. *Taiseki Ji*, the Main Temple of the Soka Gakkai, cost its members the stupendous sum of 36 billion yen. I am sure that the 36 billion yen temple, in which marble is used even in toilets, will certainly impress people! The 36 billion yen temple will give the adherents much needed self-identity. 'I belong to the great temple!' 'I worship St Nichiren in the great temple!' 'Look at the great temple we built!' 'Who are we? We are the ones who built a 36 billion yen temple!' . . . What an impressive self-identity! But it is expensive too.

I am sure that the 36 billion yen temple is very much visible. 'Nor do men light a lamp and put it under a bushel, but on a stand,

and it gives light to all in the house' (Matt. 5.15). A 36 billion yen
lamp! In contrast, the delicate movements of our mind are invisible.
'Now the works of the flesh are plain: immorality, impurity, licen-
tiousness, idolatry, sorcery, enmity, strife, jealousy, anger,
selfishness, dissension, party spirit, envy, drunkenness, carousing,
and the like. ... But the fruit of the Spirit is love, joy, peace,
patience, kindness, goodness, faithfulness, gentleness, self-
control. ...' (Gal. 5.19–23). Our invisible life is simply overwhelmed by the impressive appearance of the visible religion. The
36 billion yen lamp does not illuminate the spiritual problems of
man. It will, on the contrary, overshadow them. It will ironically
paralyse human spiritual sensitivity. It is not easy to think about
the hidden works of the flesh or fruits of the spirit in the marble
toilet!

I am tempted to think that the 36 billion yen temple is an
expression of inner insecurity. A building is at least 'tangible' and
'secure'. It will be there, not for eternity but for some time.... A
mere mention of this enormous sum creates an atmosphere of objec-
tive prestige. Inner insecurity yearns for this kind of external
prestige.

A temple is 'sacred space'. It is a symbol for 'people standing
before God'. The English word *profanity* comes from *pro* (before)
and *fanum* (temple), that is, 'outside the temple'. What does 'people
standing before God' mean? It means that the people examine
seriously their own social responsibility. When people are disturbed
by social injustice, they are in truth confronted by the presence and
power of the sacred. They are in the temple then. 'You shall not
hate your brother in your heart, but you shall reason with your
neighbour, lest you bear sin because of him, you shall not take
vengeance or bear any grudge against the sons of your own people,
but you shall love your neighbour as yourself: I am the Lord' (Lev.
19.17,18). This great passage expresses the *meaning* of the temple.
The temple is related to our inner life – our 'heart'. The sacredness
of the temple locates the power that aims to eliminate 'hate'. There
must not be vengeance and grudge when we are confronted by the
sacred. The whole message of the temple is summarized in the
sentence; 'you shall love your neighbour as yourself'. In the temple
this commandment is heard together with the concluding divine
declaration; 'I am the Lord'.

'I am the Lord.' This means 'I am holy'. Because the Lord is
holy his command 'you shall love your neighbour as yourself' is to
be taken seriously. God is saying that his name will be mentioned
in our act of loving our neighbour as ourselves. 'You shall not take
the name of the Lord your God in vain. ...' (Exod. 20.7). You shall

not waste God's name by ignoring your neighbour. If such is the meaning of the temple then the five commandments of the Ten Commandments (the sixth to the tenth commandment) describe our experience of the sacred. Let me quote here from Canaan Banana's paraphrasing of the Ten Commandments:

6. Thou shalt not deny your brother his dignity, for to despise a man is to murder him.

7. Thou shalt not prostitute your integrity for personal gain, but invest your life in the cause of humanity.

8. Thou shalt not live by the exploitation of others; but shall strive for the sharing of prosperity.

9. Thou shalt neither classify nor humiliate your neighbour, for racism perverts the Soul.

10. Thou shalt not be jealous of the achievements of your Comrade, but rejoice in them always.

'You shall love your neighbour as yourself.' This is the meaning of responsibility. The concept of responsibility and that of sacredness are intimately related. Irresponsibility is profanity. Wild pursuit after private wealth and power is profane activity since it is irresponsible. Such irresponsibility produces alienation; '... We seek more and more privacy, and feel more and more alienated and lonely when we get it'.

The meaningful life of which the Bible speaks is in the direction of human relationship instead of expensive self-enlargement. It is in the direction of the meaning of the temple. Jesus Christ fulfils the sacred intention of the temple. His attention is focused on the restoration of the covenant relationship between God and man, and man and man. This relationship is restored by him. He is the Living Temple. His name means; 'You shall love your neighbour as yourself: I am the Lord'. He is Responsible Life. This is the tradition we received from the apostles. The apostolic tradition is inexpensive in terms of hard-cash. It is 'expensive' in terms of love and self-giving. Inexpensive yet resourceful apostolic style of life. Both technology and temple must be influenced by this great tradition. Profanity is expensive.

None is righteous, no, not one . . .   *Romans 3.10*

All of us will die someday. This is the inescapable fact about human life. Upon this earth of ours we do not find even one person today who is two hundred years old. 'The years of our life are threescore and ten, or even by reason of strength fourscore; yet their span is but toil and trouble; they are soon gone, and we fly away' (Ps. 90.19). Death comes universally to all people, including those in the highest and lowest stations of life. 'You were made from soil and you will become soil again' (TEV).

'Decay is inherent in all component things! Work out your salvation with diligence!' This was the last word of the Buddha. What is this salvation?

> When the Exalted One died, the venerable Anuruddha, at the moment of his passing away from existence, uttered these stanzas:
>
> When he who from all craving want was free,
> Who to Nirvana's tranquil state had reached,
> When the great sage finished his span of life,
> No grasping struggle vexed that steadfast heart!
>
> All resolute, and with unshaken mind,
> He calmly triumphed o'er the pain of death.
> E'en as a bright flame dies away, so was
> The last emancipation of his heart.[34]

The Buddha observed the suffering (*dukkha*) of man. 'Birth is suffering; decay is suffering; illness is suffering; death is suffering. Presence of objects we hate is suffering; separation from objects we love is suffering; not to obtain what we desire is suffering.' This is the first of the Four Noble Truths of the Enlightened One. These are simple and powerful words. According to him all this suffering derives from human greed (*tanha*). Our greedy attachment to life makes our life miserable. If we were not lustfully attached to life then death would not be suffering. Such is the diagnosis given by the Buddha. The therapy of the Buddha then is concentrated on the elimination of greed. If greed is eradicated suffering will be automatically eliminated. He goes one step further; human greed comes from human ignorance (*avijja*). Ignorance here means the state of mind which does not understand the painful relationship between greed and suffering. Ignorance (*avijja*) produces greed (*tanha*) and greed delivers man to suffering *(dukkha)*. This is the fundamental message of Buddhism.

'None is righteous, no, not one. . . .' (Romans 3.10). The Buddha would say; 'None is free from greed, no, not one. . . .' In this syndrome of ignorance, greed and suffering, there is 'neither Jew nor Greek, there is neither slave nor free, there is neither male nor female'. This is the universalism of Buddhism. In this Buddhism stands against the traditional Hindu world of caste system. The Hindu world was divided into four castes; the priests (*brahmin*), the ruler-warriors (*kshatriya*), the merchant and farmers (*vaishya*) and the servants (*shudra*). The people below the servants are called the 'fifth class' (*pancama*). Later they were called untouchables, outcastes, depressed classes or scheduled castes. The term 'scheduled castes' has been used by the Indian Government since 1932 and appears in the Constitution.

Buddhism challenges the caste mentality of the Hindu world.

No brahman is such by birth.
No outcaste is such by birth.
An outcaste is such by his deeds.
A brahman is such by his deeds.
(*Sutta Nipata*, verse 136)

Behind this verse is the profound observation of the Buddha on the greed of man. There is, as it were, 'the unity of mankind' in that every man is greedy. We must not hastily react, saying that this Buddhist observation is negative. It points to a very realistic understanding of man. On this realism, Buddhism has been able to build more elaborate religious systems.

Nirvana, the state of 'the flame of greed blown out', is salvation. It is the state of absolute tranquility. It is undecaying. Personally I have no way of appreciating *nirvana*. How do I feel when I go into the realm of absolute tranquility? But I am interested to see 'the flame of greed blown out' while we are living here and now. Struggle against our greediness is a frustrating, yet vitally important, undertaking. I appreciate the universalism and realism of Buddhism.

39 A Sign for You: A Babe

And this will be sign for you: you will find a babe wrapped in swaddling cloths and lying in a manger.

Luke 2.12

The babe lies in a manger. On a make-shift bed. So Luke tells us. And adds, 'because there was no room for them in the inn'.

'And the Word became flesh and "tented" (dwelt) among us' says John (1.14). 'Foxes have holes, and the birds of the air have nests', said Jesus himself, 'but the Son of Man has nowhere to lay his head' (Matt. 8.20).

The title Pharaoh means 'Great House'. The name Jesus means 'The Lord is Salvation'. It is good that the name does not mean 'Little House'. The conflict between Jesus and Pharaoh is not one between the great house and the small house. It is between the salvation which comes from the Lord and the self-glorification and self-enlargement which Pharaoh represents.

'There was no place for them in the inn' – that is a little difficult to understand. There was no place because there were too many people, but wouldn't there be somebody among them who would help a pregnant woman? Perhaps people were as busy then as they are today with their own concerns and comforts.

There are 650,000 Koreans living in Japan at present. They are the victims of indifference and discrimination. There is no room for them in the inn.

The Treaty of Waitangi was signed in 1840. With the signing of it, 'sovereignty' over New Zealand passed to Queen Victoria. The native Maoris had little understanding of the Anglo-Saxon concept of Law. Their land – that is their life – was now taken away from them. They have become strangers in their own land. There is no place for them in the inn, in their own inn.

Like the Koreans in Japan and the Maoris in New Zealand today, Christ the lord must make do with a make-shift arrangement. He goes to a manger, a trough in which fodder is kept for cattle. From the manger, not from the Great House, the babe encounters the world – God himself encounters all mankind.

The babe is protected. He is wrapped in swaddling cloths and he lies in an eating trough. It is sub-standard protection. With that kind of protection the babe is exposed, open both to those who come to worship (the shepherds and wise men) and to those who come to destroy (Herod, the man of the Great House). Anyone may approach the babe. He lives a 'tented' life. He does not build a wall around himself. He does not arm himself. The sign of swaddling cloths and manger means that he mingles with people. He is free, with the freedom of the manger, not of the Great House. 'And the Word became flesh and dwelt among us, full of grace and truth. . . .' (John 1.14). No power can destroy this strange sign. 'The light shines in the darkness, and the darkness has not overcome it' (John 1.5).

This babe – God incarnate – is the sign against human insensitivity to the need of others. When we do not provide room for others, we worship at the shrine of Baal who is the sign of insensitivity. Once we have got our rooms we forget the needs of those who have no room in the inn. That is self-glorification and self-enlargement. And that is sin.

One of the most terrifying expressions of insensitivity in our day is Global Militarism. It is steadily destroying the health and integrity (*shalom*) of mankind. In 1977 the Third World spent the staggering sum of 40.1 billion for the procurement of arms. Weapons are filling up every human space. They come in the order of A.B.C. (Atomic, Biological, Chemical). And the more armed we are, the more threatened we feel. An outcome of our sin is insensitivity to the needs of others.

Jesus Christ stands against our insensitivity. He not only stands against it; he also heals us. The sign of swaddling cloths and the manger extends to the events of the cross and resurrection. By loving us to the utmost, Jesus Christ heals us.

Look closely at him . . . in the manger, on the cross and outside the tomb.

40   The Holy in Our Naming and Misnaming

. . . . whatever the man called every living creature, that was its name. The man gave names to all cattle, and to the birds of the air, and to every beast of the field.   *Genesis 2.19,20*

Adam – humankind – creates meaning in his environment and lives in the network of meaning and value which he has made. This, he does, as an intelligent person, in the naming of things, old and new. This obnoxious flying insect he named mosquito. This powder that kills the mosquito he named DDT. This emaciating fever caused by the mosquito he named malaria. And this remarkable drug to fight against malaria he named quinine. His naming activity knows no end from mosquito to proton-neutron to 'Greater East Asian Co-Prosperity Sphere' to Maoism.

The naming man is engaged in a holy act. To name is to substantiate. To name is to 'hallow'. To name this white stuff sugar is to 'hallow' sugar. To name this person woman is to 'hallow' the woman. The moment of naming is the moment of reality. Naming makes real.

Man's ability to name, however, is tragically his ability to *misname*. Because he can name, he can misname. Outside of 'Eden' naming always involves the risk of misnaming. When man names he gives meaning to cosmos. The cosmos is enlivened by him and for him. When man misnames he creates a 'mis-cosmos', a chaos. Of course, there is orderliness and chaos apart from man's naming. Whether or not man names it the sun rises in the east every morning. Whether man misnames it or not there is chaos in the cancer that grows in the most delicate units of life. Perhaps chaos is the normal form of existence and orderliness is an exception. Yet . . . human well-being does depend on how we name things. What happened when the military fanatics of Japan named the 'Greater East Asia Co-Prosperity Sphere'? What happened when the emperor of Japan was called *Akitsu Mikami* (God made visible)?

I find the following paragraphs in Karl Marx's *Capital*:

> The manufacture of lucifer matches dates from 1833, from the discovery of the method of applying phosphorus to the match itself. Since 1845 this manufacture has rapidly developed in England. . . . Half the workers are children under thirteen, and young persons under eighteen. The manufacture is on account of its unhealthiness and unpleasantness in such bad odour that only the most miserable part of the labouring class, half-starved widows and so forth, deliver up their children to it, 'The ragged, half-starved, untaught children'. . . . 270 were under 18, 50 under 10, 10 only 8, and 5 only 6 years old. A range of the working day from 12 to 14 or 15 hours, night-labour, irregular mealtimes, meals for the most part taken in the very workrooms that are pestilent with phosphorus. Dante would have found the worst horrors of his Inferno surpassed in this manufacture.[35]

This is not cosmos. This is, indeed, Inferno-chaos. To 'name' such inhuman condition as 'necessary for the sake of economic development' is demonic 'misnaming' – mistreatment of the human person. Don't we have many 'lucifer match industries' in South East Asia today?

The infamous prison appropriately named the 'tiger's cage' in the South Vietnam of Thieu was an iron bar box of 2.5 metres square and 1.5 metres high. In this iron cage were jammed ten to seventeen prisoners. Their hands and feet were chained crosswise day and night. Drinking water was given in the same container used for human excrement. Here no human space was given. Space means freedom and responsibility to man. When space is denied humanity is denied. It is a picture of a particularly insidious man-made chaos. Man cannot live in the 'tiger's cage' as man.

A sense of human dignity rejects the 'lucifer match industry' and the 'tiger's cage'. Naming he declares creatively 'I am human', and misnaming he declares destructively 'I am human'. I am human! Is this insight? Is this religious conviction? Is it a philosophical conclusion? Committee decision? . . . It is the voice of man in his *de profundis*. He cannot quite understand from where this affirmation comes. But it comes from within. In it is the possibility of man's health, happiness and future. It is a sacred affirmation. In this sacred affirmation is found the universal context in which damnation (chaos) and salvation (cosmos) can be meaningfully discussed.

Man – Adam – does not have to be of a certain race, of certain education, of certain income, of certain ability, of certain religion. Adam is Adam whether he is influenced by the *Qur'an*, the *Lotus Sutra*, the *Bhagavad Gita* or the *Bible*. There is neither Christian Adam, nor Buddhist nor Moslem Adam. Adam is simply Adam, human being. (' . . . adham occurs well over five hundred times in the Old Testament with the meaning "man" or "mankind". This generic term is used only rarely as a proper name for the first man.')[36] He is 'dust of the earth' (humbleness) plus 'breath of God' (awareness of the presence of God : Genesis 2.7) This combination is the substance and structure of human dignity. It is this that refuses to be insulted.

'You are untouchable' and all the many variations of that statement are a denial of this human dignity:

'Keep to the side of the road, oh low-caste vermin!' he suddenly heard someone shouting at him. 'Why don't you call, you swine, and announce your approach! Do you know you have touched me and defiled me, cock-eyed son of a bowlegged scorpion! Now I will have to go and take a bath to purify myself. And it was a new dhoti and shirt I put on this morning'![37]

The man tragically thinks that he can produce cosmos again simply by changing a dhoti and shirt after he has himself engaged in such violent misnaming. He can. But that cosmos would be a false cosmos, far more insidious than an obvious chaos. The sense of the holy in us tells us so.

The holy is an inspiration which demands full meaning for 'I am human'. The holy is the mysterious heat that keeps the 'inalienable rights of man' warm and viable. Theology in the Adam context must be sensitively in dialogue with this heat. Adam is neither in *nirvana* or in 'Eden'. He is engaged in naming and misnaming. In this activity the holy is experienced. The holy is not a tranquil or a detached concept. The holy is present in our confusing history in which we name and misname.

41 'Dust and Ashes' Self-Identity

And the Lord said, 'If I find at Sodom fifty righteous in the city, I will spare the whole place for their sake'. Abraham answered, 'Behold, I have taken upon myself to speak to the Lord, I who am but dust and ashes. Suppose five of the fifty righteous are lacking? Wilt thou destroy the whole city for lack of five?' . . . Then he said, 'Oh let not the Lord be angry, and I will speak again but this once. Suppose ten are found there.' He answered, 'For the sake of ten I will not destroy it'. And the Lord went his way, when he had finished speaking to Abraham; and Abraham returned to his place.   *Genesis 18.26–33*

Abraham pleads with God for the salvation of the people of Sodom. Persistently, intelligently and rationally he 'bargains' with God. All the while he never forgets that he is 'but dust and ashes'. He knows that if such conversation can continue it is through the sheer mercy of God. The Lord accepts the form and principle of Abraham's argument. The 'Judge of all the earth' (v.25) goes along with Abraham all the way from fifty to ten. Abraham stopped at ten. He must have thought that the negotiation was satisfactorily concluded for the sake of the people of Sodom.

The story is triggered off by Abraham's personal concern over the fate of the sinful city of Sodom. Sodom is a city of social injustice, exploitation, human indignity, slum-life, sexual chaos, prostitution, good-life-for-few, bad-life-for-many, racial discrimination, oppressive government, bribery, political prisoners, denial of human rights, . . . Abraham speaks for the city whose sin is 'very grave' (v. 20).

How does one intercede in such hopeless situation? Between the holy God and the unholy city stood Abraham who felt himself to be 'but dust and ashes'. What an intercessor. Mr Dust-and-ashes pleading for the salvation of the wicked city. Behold, he succeeds. Not in the holy city but in the unholy city of Sodom – in the Sodom context! – so the biblical writers show us both the forgiving mind of God and the spiritual stature of the father of many nations (Gen. 17.5). He conducts his negotiation from a position of weakness. In tradition of biblical teaching this is wise.

Abraham decides to walk right into the 'secular' problem. Strangely his self-identity as 'dust and ashes' provides him spiritual, psychological and intellectual energy to wrestle with the problem of the sinful city. Notice that Abraham takes the lead in the discussion with the Judge of all the earth. What he is discussing is full of social and political implications. In his negotiation with the Lord he experiences political power. Yes. This story is a political story in the sense that it seeks a workable just compromise. The German scholar Rudolf Otto, in his celebrated book, *The Idea of the Holy*,[38] names the feeling of Abraham, 'but dust and ashes' a 'creature-feeling'. 'Creature-feeling' sounds to us 'religious' and 'pious'. But the right kind of creature-feeling can produce political and social power. It represents the knowledge of one's limitation in ability and holiness. Such a knowledge is creative. A wrong creature-feeling is a feeling of self-rejection and despair. Such creature-feeling cannot contribute creativity to the human community.

The religious person can be timid and negative. But he can also be bold and positive. He may wish to spend his life retired in the forest. But he can as well be a most articulate person in the crowded streets of the city. Religion can be narcotic in its influence upon man. But religion can be instead the source of awakening of one's social responsibility. Religious life is ambiguous. It can make man sensitive or insensitive to the problem of society.

Abraham was not under the influence of opium. He was under the sense of impending historical and social crisis. As he watched the city of Sodom he sensed that the time of judgment upon it was come. He was fully awake. He was the 'awakened one'. In the context of the sinful city he became a *buddha*. In his awareness that he is 'but dust and ashes' he stands before the Lord. He has a healthy self-identity in the presence of the Creator.

No one can bribe such a man. The man of 'but dust and ashes' is not interested in personal gain. No one can threaten him. Such a man is fearless. He is free. He can live for others.

In one of many books he has written, the Japanese Zen scholar D. T. Suzuki tells us about an incident which made him critical of Christianity. He says that one day he met a Christian missionary who was carrying a number of keys about on his belt. This 'ordinary' sight impressed the young Suzuki that this person must be irreligious. Religious persons must be free from the very need of having keys. Key represents attachment. It means self-protection and self-encirclement. It creates a barrier to prevent genuine religious communication with others. Here, Suzuki, in his own way, tells us the secret power of the religious person who is able to see himself as 'but dust and ashes'.

Abraham's 'dust and ashes' self-identity is theological. It is neither neurotic nor negative. This theological self-identity has political power.

42   Ethnocentric Pride

Then the Lord God formed man of dust from the ground, and breathed into his nostrils the breath of life; and man became a living being.

Genesis 2.7

The official report of the Fourth Assembly of the World Council of Churches which met in Uppsala in 1968 provides this definition of racism:

> By racism we mean ethnocentric *pride* in one's own racial group and preference for the distinctive characteristics of that group; belief that these characteristics are fundamentally biological in nature and are thus transmitted to succeeding generations; strong negative feeling towards other groups who do not share these characteristics coupled with the thrust to discriminate against and exclude the outgroup from full participation in the life of the community.[39]

Both Japanese and Koreans are Asians. But 650,000 Koreans in Japan today are subjected to brutal discrimination by the Japanese people.

The Koreans in Japan became 'foreigners' in 1952 after the signing of the San Francisco Peace Treaty. They were stripped of their former Japanese nationality without freedom to choose their nationality. The Japan Korea Treaty of 1965 did make some provision for 'permanent residence' – but that was not 'permanent residence rights' in the strict sense of the word, as the rights can be withdrawn any time when the conditions attached are broken. This is, in fact, another way of controlling the Koreans. Koreans in Japan are also denied social security and many other social benefits, although they pay the same taxes as Japanese. . . .[40]

Unfortunately some form of racism is to be found in every country today. Let me quote from the forty-page pamphlet: *The Queensland Aborigines Act and Regulations 1971, Written by the Black Resource Centre Collective 1976, So that Anyone can Read and Understand These Acts*:

A lot of white people don't know about the racist laws that oppress Aboriginals and Torres Strait Islanders in Queensland. These Acts were started off in 1897. When white people first came to this land they had guns which they used on blacks. They brought disease such as Syphilis, TB, Leprosy, Scabies, Gonorrhoea, Smallpox etc. When they realized that black people were not going to die out they decided to set up Reserve Settlements. They rounded up the tribal people. They took them away from their own land and took them to places like Palm Island, Cherbourg, Woorabinda, Yarrbah, and split up the tribes and families to create confusion.

White Managers were set up on the Reserves to govern the people instead of the people controlling their own lives. The white farmers and graziers realized that they could get cheap black labour from the reserves and no-one could force them to pay proper wages and to give good conditions. Black people were forbidden to speak their own languages and have their own culture. The people were forbidden to leave the Reserves to live their own ways. They were forbidden to have a good education but were taught white man's history which told them that Captain Cook discovered Australia in 1770. (Which is *bull*, because Aboriginal people have lived here for more than 40,000 years.) They were taught that black people were not as important as white people and still are taught that today.

These laws and conditions still exist today. These laws are like Apartheid in South Africa but worse, because white people don't know about the Queensland Aboriginal and Torres Strait Islanders Acts and don't support blacks in the struggle to smash these racist laws.

The unfathomable processes of nature produced what we are. We are humankind. We live a conscious life. We sense our social responsibility. We are able to stand at a distance from ourselves and look at ourselves. Our understanding of our environment is constantly increasing. We are probing many areas; sociology, biology, psychology, history, politics, physics, science, medicine, economics, government. . . . We have harnessed nuclear energy for our use. A quite remarkable humankind. But . . . we have not emancipated ourselves from the destructive power of racism. We might have made 'unprecedented progress' in many areas, but we have miserably failed to place 'ethnocentric pride' under our control. Our ethnocentric pride remains untamed.

Can we ignore the issue of ethnocentric pride? Is this an esoteric subject?

We cannot overlook this problem since it is to do with the basic meaning of 'to be human'. 'To be human' is different from 'to be animal'. It is different from 'to be thing'. Racism is a devastating insult to human dignity. It does not attack the periphery. It injures the centre of man. It desacralizes that which is sacred in him. It is a blasphemy against the deepest level of human identity. Man is made from soil and he will become soil again. Man is humble in his beginning and in his end. This is, however, a half story about man. Man began to live, according to the Bible, by the breath of God. He is inspired by God. Racism insults this inspiration of God which is in man. The presence of the breath of God is the source of man's human dignity.

Racism produces enormous misery and destruction within the family of humanity. All of us are asked, in the name of human dignity, to look at the tragic dimension and reality of racism in the world today. The Fifth Assembly of the World Council of Churches (Nairobi 1975) speaks in its report about 'Racism in Churches'. It is a matter of great urgency for every Christian to reflect upon the following quotation:

> To our shame, Christian churches around the world are all too often infected by racism, overt and covert. Examples of it include the following:
> (a) churches and congregations have been and are still being organized along racially exclusive lines;
> (b) congregations welcome to their fellowship warmly those who are like the majority of its members, but easily reject those who are different;

(c) many argue that they are free of racism as if its reality could be undone by ignoring it;

(d) churches frequently contribute to the psychological conditioning of the racially oppressed so that they will not sense the racism imposed upon them;

(e) they are more willing to support struggles against racism far from home than to face the racism which is practised on their doorstep;

(f) churches often reflect the racially prejudiced attitudes of their governments, their elites, and self-pretensions, while presuming that their own attitudes arise out of Christian faith;

(g) in leadership privileges and in programmatic priorities churches tend too easily to indulge in racism without even recognizing it.[41]

This observation at Nairobi comes from 'Fundamental Convictions' which were read at the Assembly:

Racism is a sin against God and against fellow human beings. It is contrary to the justice and the love of God revealed in Jesus Christ. It destroys the human dignity of both the racist and the victim. When practised by Christians it denies the very faith we profess and undoes the credibility of the Church and its witness to Jesus Christ. Therefore, we condemn racism in all its forms both inside and outside the Church.[42]

43 Insult or Dignity?

Not every one who says to me 'Lord, Lord' shall enter the kingdom of heaven, but he who does the will of my Father who is in heaven.
Matthew 7.21

'Vehicles and Dogs Prohibited' – says the signpost at the entrance of the Dunedin Botanical Garden. I say to myself; 'prohibited is a big word!'

The dog is man's oldest animal friend. Companionship between man and dog has long been mutually satisfying. On the sheep farms of New Zealand, the dog is a faithful and hard worker. Yet the Old

Testament writers do not speak kindly of the dog. Job 30.1 mentions a sheep dog. But it is more a scavenger than a clean working dog. Dogs eat unclean things. 'You shall be men consecrated to me; therefore you shall not eat any flesh that is torn by beasts in the field; you shall cast it to the dogs' (Exod. 22.31). Or how about this! 'You shall not bring the hire of a harlot, or the wages of a dog, into the house of the Lord your God in payment for any vow; for both of these are an abomination to the Lord your God' (Deut. 23.18). 'Dog' here seems to mean male temple prostitute. Poor dog. I wonder why the Old Testament does not speak kindly of the dog.

The vehicle is an extension of the wheel, one of the oldest and most brilliant of human technological devices. Some suggest that the 'companionship' between the wheel and man may go back 5000 years. To carry (*vehere*, – hence vehicle) things the wheel was an epoch making invention. From baby-carriage to jumbo jet wheels are required. The jumbo jet must come down to the ground. On the ground wheels, not wings, are needed.

Two of the oldest of human acquaintances – dog and vehicle – are prohibited to go into the garden. The reason is obvious. If dogs run around – and there are protected ducks in the pond – and motorcycles and bicycles crisscross in the garden, how can the citizens, old, young and babies, enjoy the peace of the garden?

So Dunedin Botanical Garden excludes dogs and vehicles. Once Bund Park in the European section of Shanghai had a signpost at the entrance reading, 'No Chinese and dogs allowed'. I have read somewhere that the young Mao Tse-Tung saw it and could not forget this insult all through his life. 'No dogs and vehicles' is not insulting. But the one in Shanghai is a completely different story. It attacks the holiness of the human person. It insults human dignity. *Wia mai ki au he aha te mea nui, maku e ki aut 'He Tangata, he tangata, he tangata'* ('Inquire of me what thing is the most important; I will answer, "Man, Man, Man"!' New Zealand Maori saying).

I have not seen the infamous signpost myself. Mao Tse-Tung has eliminated it. I think it must not have been as big as Lenin's poster in front of the Moscow International Airport or Chang Kai Shek's image in front of Taipei International Airport. It must have been a relatively small signpost, but this small signpost did enormous harm to the integrity of the 'Christian West'. The human mind and emotion can be expressed in symbols as elaborate and extensive as Borobudur and Angkor Wat, or as small as the Shanghai signpost. I wonder whether Christian missionaries in Shanghai at that time saw the signpost. They would have noticed immediately if the sign said, for instance, 'No Americans and dogs allowed'! This points to the secret mechanism of insensitivity which is working at the depth of our egoistic mind.

It was in China that the signpost 'No Chinese and dogs allowed' was placed. China is the land of the Chinese people. What a strange message the signpost carried. At once my thought goes to the people of the scheduled castes in India. The term *scheduled castes*, which has been used by the Indian Government since 1932, means outcastes. Gandhi called them *Harijans*, 'Children of God'. According to the 1971 Census of India there are about 80 million scheduled castes in the total population of 550 million. The scheduled castes make up 15% of the population. Harijans are Indians. But wherever they go within India they see the visible and invisible restrictions which say 'Harijans not allowed'.

V. T. Rajshekar Shetty, a correspondent of the '*Indian Express*', Bangalore, India writes:

> What then is the basic issue? Untouchability is a problem that has come down the centuries as part of our fourfold *chatur varna* (caste system) – *Brahmana, Kshatriya, Vaishya, Shudra*. The untouchables are called panchamas because they are outside the caste system. Hence, they are aptly called outcastes. Being at the bottom of the caste pyramid they are the last and the lowliest, socially the meanest and economically the poorest. Their very touch or even a look leads to pollution.
>
> Such a pyramid is something unheard of in any other part of the world. The caste system is the quintessence of the Hindu genius. Like the Egyptian pyramids built by the Pharaohs, the Hindu caste pyramid is ageless and deathless. Wonder of all wonders![43]

The untouchable is condemned to the meanest professions, such as scavenging, garbage cleaning, sweeping, removing dead cattle, shoemaking. He cannot worship Hindu gods and cannot touch Hindu scriptures. B. R. Ambedkar writes:

> The Romans had their slaves, the Spartans their helots, the British their villains, the Americans their negroes and the Germans their Jews. So the Hindus have their untouchables. But none of these can be said to have been called upon to face a fate which is worse than the fate which pursues the Untouchables. Slavery, serfdom, villeinage have all vanished. But untouchability still exists and bids fair to last as long as Hinduism will last. The untouchable is worse off than a Jew. The sufferings of the Jews are of his own creation. Not so are the sufferings of the untouchables. They are the result of a cold calculating Hinduism which is not less sure in its effect in producing misery than brute

force is. The Jew is despised but is not denied opportunities to grow. The untouchable is not merely despised but is denied all opportunities to rise. Yet nobody seems to take any notice of the untouchables – much less espouse their cause.[44]

The Christian Conference of Asia at its ad hoc meeting on Race and Minority Issues in Asia held in Hong Kong, March 1977, gave this working definition of minority: 'A minority is a group of people who, because of their physical or cultural characteristics, are singled out from others in the society in which they live for differential and unequal treatment, and who therefore regard themselves as objects of collective discrimination'. This implies the existence of a dominant group with higher social privileges and powers. The Hong Kong paper points out that the minority is usually subjected to four kinds of oppression; geographical, economic, political and sociocultural.

At the Anglican Maori Mission Centre in Auckland, New Zealand, a workshop in race and minority issues was held in November 1978 sponsored again by the Christian Conference of Asia. It was a most unusual international gathering of representatives of minority groups: Aborigines, Pacific Islanders from Australia, Harijans and Tribals from India, Chinese from Indonesia, *Burakumin* and Koreans from Japan, Tamils from Malaysia, Maoris and Pacific Islanders from New Zealand, Christians from Pakistan, Cultural minorities and Muslims from the Philippines, and Tamils from Sri Lanka. In all forty of them stayed together for one week and shared their experiences, strategies and theology. These are the people for whom a 'No Dogs and . . . allowed' signpost has been erected.

Pondering on their discussions I made the following observations:

1. To be human means to live peacefully *upon the land.* Taking away land from the people by force or trickery is an insult to human dignity. 'The missionaries asked us to look up to heaven; while we looked the land was taken from beneath our feet', said the Maoris in New Zealand. While we are not to worship the land or the fertility of the land, we value the land as the carrier of the sacred memory of the people.

2. To be human means to live peacefully *with our neighbour.* When we injure our neighbour we are destroying his human dignity. This is the serious meaning of injury. When we injure others in this sense we are also destroying our own human dignity. Brutal exploitation and oppression erodes our human dignity. The biblical God is very much concerned about this injury. He comes to us with his judgment and healing and he moves us to participate in his work of healing.

3. To be human means to *live with God*. God is concerned about human integrity and social justice. He is the source of our human dignity.

'The will of my Father who is in heaven' is clear. Injury which is being perpetrated upon the minorities by the dominant groups must be terminated. All kinds of 'infamous signposts' and unjust laws must be removed. The rights of the minorities must be upheld and their human dignity must be restored and protected.

'Not every one who says to me "Lord, Lord", shall enter the kingdom of heaven, but he who does the will of my Father who is in heaven' (Matt. 7.21). The theme of exclusion is spoken here personally. The primary importance is in doing the will of God. 'Entering into the kingdom of heaven' is secondary. We are exhorted to be concerned with the primary, then the secondary will follow. Obedience to the words of Jesus will make us responsible in this world. We are not threatened. We are encouraged. We are invited to do joyously what the Father who is in heaven wants us to do. The Father wants us to eliminate all human sinful arrangements which injure others. Jan Milic Lochman, the Czechoslovakian theologian writes;

> . . . But this, precisely, is the mission of the Christian: to seek and see the face of Jesus Christ over each and every man. There is a beautiful saying of Luther: 'To receive Jesus Christ in every man and to be Jesus Christ to every man.' This means that for the sake of Jesus Christ none may ever be excluded from our common humanity. To look for this bond when defending ourselves, when contradicting, when facing the opponent – and to love even the enemy – this is Christian witness.[45]

We are called to become 'Jesus Christ' to every man. Such is the meaning of Matthew 7.21. It is a call to bear witness. Jesus Christ says that the doers of the will of God shall enter the kingdom of heaven. The life and ministry of Jesus was focused on the removal of personal alienation and social injustice from the world. He was the doer. In him the kingdom of God has come.

The suffering of minorities is a pervasive reality. Often we are tempted to think of this subject as a peripheral one. It is not peripheral since God himself is emphatically involved in it himself. This issue then is at the heart of our social life today. It is there we find the judgment and hope of God.

But Peter said, 'I have no silver and gold, but I give you what I have; in the name of Jesus Christ of Nazareth, walk'.   *Acts 3.6*

Enough . . . abundance . . . saturation. Three words come to me as I walk through Singapore's endless shopping complexes. I know what they mean and I ponder on their fascination for me. They all suggest plentifulness. I like plentifulness. I am happy to see a full bowl of steaming rice in front of me. I want to have enough, and if possible an abundance of this world's good. But saturation, I feel, is a problem.

I may find it convenient to have ten telephones in my home, but then, again, I may find it simply too many. The convenience of not having to move when the telephone rings may be overcome by the persistent ringing which I could not escape. I should feel that I had planned poorly. If my telephones were to show off my status, I should soon be dissatisfied with their ineffectiveness. And I should feel within myself a touch of irresponsibility in terms of stewardship – a touch of greediness. Saturation culture can be a wild, uncontrolled, undisciplined culture. It can be . . . and it tends to be.

Abundance is different from saturation, though the border between them may be indistinct and too easily crossed. As I see it, man possesses *abundance* with a disciplined mind and a sense of gratitude. It is a religious approach to plenty. Discipline makes it possible for him to enjoy plenty without becoming a slave to his things. Perhaps there will be two telephones, conveniently placed. Gratitude generates spiritual vitality and creativity. The telephones will be used to good purpose and for meaningful communication. Gratitude is to acknowledge that the plenty we enjoy is a gift from God. The prophet Hosea (2.8) makes the point clearly, though in a negative way. 'She would never acknowledge that I am the one who gave her the grain, the wine, the olive oil, and all the silver and gold that she used in the worship of Baal.' To acknowledge that plenty comes from God (of responsible growth) not from Baal (of irresponsible growth) is the beginning of abundance.

Television, whether in Tokyo or San Francisco or Singapore, is a constant reminder to us of the saturation culture. At any time of the day or night, at a flick of the switch, its message is there. 'You need this. . . .' 'You want that. . . .' 'Take advantage of the special offer!' Religious television is not free from the spirit of advertising.

It, too, seems to advertise its goods, calling attention to numbers of satisfied listeners and offering its advice pamphlets for a 'gift' or a price. The 'evangelists' seem to sanction the saturation culture. They give us the impression that Jesus Christ accepts saturation. 'In the name of Japanese saturation', I seem to hear, 'I order you to get up and walk!'

It all sounds dynamic. It professes to carry a message that is helpful and healing. But it harbours a hidden danger. Man does not and cannot get up and walk in the name of saturation. All kinds of products do not solve human problems. Nor do 'how to' pamphlets. The American people know this. The Japanese people know this. American anxiety arises out of the saturation culture.

Yet the most idealistic of us must admit that we do need 'silver and gold' in order to live a humanly adequate life. Peter said, 'I have no silver or gold'. But the Good Samaritan in the parable of the Lord was able to pick up the medical bill for his neighbour. Obviously he had the 'silver and gold' he needed in order to be of help. What, then, does Peter's protest mean? Why is 'I have no money at all' a basic characteristic of the apostolic personality? Were the apostles impoverished? No! They lived an abundant life. Gratitude to God, gratitude to Jesus of Nazareth was so intense within them that they had their own apostolic understanding of 'enough'. For Peter 'I have no silver and gold' means 'I always look at silver and gold under the overwhelming sense of gratitude to God'. Or 'what God has provided is abundant for me. I have no need for more. And I say this joyously'. This is the apostolic secret. 'I have no silver and gold' is not a legalistic formula. It is a response to grace. 'I have no silver and gold' he said. Yet he healed the man. The secret of Peter is 'gratitude' and 'Jesus'. These two combined bring healing, hope and resurrection.

The name of Jesus Christ stands for abundance. 'The Word became a human being and, full of grace and truth, lived among us. . . . Out of the fullness of his grace he has blessed us all, giving us one blessing after another (John 1.14,16 TEV). His abundance blesses us all. It enriches, it encircles us. It does not make us wild and greedy. Paul says (Phil. 2.7,8), ' . . . of his own free will he gave up all he had, and took the nature of a servant. He became like man and appeared in human likeness. He was humble and walked the path of obedience all the way to death – his death on the cross'. This is not an ordinary concept of 'fullness'. Fullness is humility, or humility is fullness. The death – the death on the cross – is 'fullness of his grace'. 'In his name walk!' Peter says. In the name of this *unusual fullness* walk.

This strange concept of 'fullness' is at the foundation of the

Christian faith. We must examine our saturation culture in the light of this fullness of Christ.

45   Let Mercy Use Technology!

> Thus says the Lord: Do justice and righteousness, and deliver from the hands of the oppressor him who has been robbed. And do no wrong or violence to the alien, the fatherless, and the widow, nor shed innocent blood in this place. For if you will indeed obey this word, then there shall enter the gates of this house kings who sit on the throne of David, riding in chariots and on horses, they, and their servants, and their people. But if you will not heed these words, I swear by myself, says the Lord, that this house shall become a desolation.   *Jeremiah 22.3–5*

'Chariots' in the Jeremiah passage, represent technology. We recognize the wheel as one of the most basic technological inventions. In Jeremiah's day, the chariot meant military might but also convenience of communication and transportation. In our own day technology means the telephone, telegram, radio, television, newspaper, car, train, planes, ... How important is the 'chariot'! But Jeremiah does not place the chariot at the beginning of the Lord's command. It appears towards the end of the paragraph. First establish social justice. Practise justice and righteousness. If you obey this word, then . . . technology – the chariot, and nature – the horse, will make a peaceful contribution to your community.

Rene Dubos writes:

> In present parlance, a society is civilized when it is affluent enough to move its outhouses indoors, to do away with physical effort, to heat and cool its homes with electric power, and to own more automobiles, freezers, telephones, and gadgets for leisure time than it really needs or can enjoy. Gentle behaviour, humane laws, limitations on war, a high level of purpose and conduct have disappeared from the concept.[46]

We take technology for granted in our everyday life. The conveniences of which Dubos speaks are accepted by us as a natural right. After all, we are civilized. But Dubos is making the same point which Jeremiah was making in the seventh century BC. Let 'gentle behaviour, humane laws, limitations on war, . . .' come first. Then technological civilization will make a meaningful and peaceful contribution to humanity. The order is of critical importance. If we take the 'chariot' before 'justice and righteousness' technology will sooner or later begin to walk by itself. Humanity will be controlled by technology. Has this already happened?

The World Fair held in Chicago in 1933, Dubos calls to our attention, exhibited a *haiku*-like slogan:

Science Finds
Industry Applies
Man Conforms

Ominous words. Already in 1933 the Fair, innocently perhaps, was pointing out the growing relationship between man and science-technology. In 1977 business in the United States spent an estimated 37 billion dollars to make people conform more completely to the products of technology. Technology can produce both good things and bad things, necessary and unnecessary things. In order to promote the sale of unnecessary things 37 billion dollars are poured into an already over-saturated life style. Technology dictates. Man follows. Why? Is it because we have ignored the order of things that Jeremiah suggested?

It is necessary to place technology within the context of social concern. In the context of social injustice, technology makes the rich ever richer and the poor ever poorer. The chariots become war chariots. Technology brings desolation to mankind. 'I swear to you that this palace will fall into ruins' (TEV).

Horses are good animals. They are beautiful and useful when the community practises justice and righteousness. But the horses (the whole animal world – nature) will turn against us if we use them in the context of social injustice. Nature cannot argue with us about social injustice, nor can it plead its own cause. But if we alienate ourselves from the animal world, from nature, we will eventually be destroyed. Not only the highly technological West, but Asia must hear this warning. Note again words of Dubos:

> Oriental civilizations give lip service to the holiness of nature, but in practice they cut down forests, erode the land, drill for coal, oil, and minerals, engage in monocultures, and pollute their environments at least as ruthlessly as do Western civilizations.[47]

That Asians are more kind to animals and to the environment is an unwarranted myth. Whether in the East or in the West, we are not to mistreat or oppress aliens, orphans and widows, or nature if we want to be happy with technology and with the world of nature.

Asia has provided us with one of the most beautiful and mean-ingful symbols of mercy. The *Bodhisattva* (*Kwan-Non* in Japanese), are Enlightened Beings in the tradition of Mahayana Buddhism. They have attained the supreme bliss of salvation for themselves. Yet they turn aside from complete salvation (*nirvana*). They post-pone their personal salvation for the sake of others. They have many hands. Some of them have even one thousand hands, each with an eye. These hands carry all kinds of objects which will be of help to man in need. The *Bodhisattva* are like well equipped ambulances, ever ready to come and help. All technological devices are at the command of mercy and concern. Mercy uses technology. Is this not a beautiful image within the Buddhist tradition? It asks us to use our vast technical skills and powers in the service of mankind not in the destruction of mankind.

Notes

1. Article on 'Holiness' in *The Interpreter's Dictionary of the Bible*, Abingdon Press 1962, vol. 2, p. 616.
2. Pascal, *Pensées*, 347.
3. P. Teilhard de Chardin, *The Phenomenon of Man*, revised edition, Fount paperbacks 1970, p. 183.
4. George F. Kennan, 'The United States and the Soviet Union 1917–1976', *Foreign Affairs*, July 1976, pp. 681f.
5. Melford E. Spiro, *Buddhism and Society*, Allen & Unwin 1971, pp. 100f.
6. Gerhard Kittel, *Theological Dictionary of the New Testament*, Eerdmans 1964, article on *aletheia*, vol. 1, p. 238.
7. Philip Noel-Baker in UNESCO, *Cultures*, vol. III, no. 4, p. 28.
8. Iwanarui Publishing House, *Sekai*, July 1978, p. 19.
9. In *Foreign Affairs*, October 1975, pp. 126 and 114f.
10. M. Eliade, *From Primitives to Zen*, Collins, and Harper & Row, New York 1967, p. 479.
11. H. R. Schlette, article on 'Missions' in *Sacramentum Mundi*, Burns & Oates 1969, vol. 4, p. 81.
12. Krister Stendahl, *Paul Among Jews and Gentiles*, SCM Press and Fortress Press 1977, p. 13.
13. Harold Lindsell in *Protestant Cross-currents in Mission*, ed., Norman A. Horner, Abingdon, Nashville 1968, pp. 61f.
14. W. Cantwell Smith, *The Meaning and End of Religion*, Macmillan 1962, reissued SPCK 1978, pp. 60f.
15. *Historical Atlas of the Religions of the World*, Isma'il R. Farūqi and David E. Sopher, Macmillan, New York, and Collier Macmillan 1974.
16. *Dhammapada Atthkatha* from *The Path of the Buddha*, ed., K. W. Morgan, Ronald Press 1956, pp. 11f.
17. Reinhold Niebuhr, *Beyond Tragedy*, Scribners 1937, preface.
18. Muraoka Tsunetsugu, *Nihon Shiso Shi Kenkyu* (Study of History of Japanese Thoughts), vol. III, pp. 53f.
19. J. Jeremias, *Rediscovering the Parables*, SCM Press and Scribners 1966, p. 181.
20. Alexander Solzhenitsyn, *The Gulag Archipelago I*, Collins/Fontana 1974, p. 175.
21. H. B. Earhart, *Religion in the Japanese Experience*, Dickenson Publishing Company 1974, pp. 207–9.
22. Ike Nobutaka, *Japan's Decision for War*, Stanford University Press 1967, p. 283.
23. See Ienaga Saburo, *Taihei-Yo Senso Shi* (History of the Pacific War), Iwanarui Publishing House, Tokyo 1968, p. 241.

24. *Jinja Mondai to Kiristo Kyo* (Issues relating to the Shinto Shrine and Christianity) ed., Tomura Masahiro, Shinkyo Publishing House, Tokyo 1976.
25. Ibid., pp. 173f.
26. Earhart, *Religion in the Japanese Experience*, pp. 10f.
27. Roger A. Johnson et al. (eds), *Critical Issues in Modern Religion*, Prentice Hall 1973, p. 224.
28. Ibid., p. 234.
29. Christian Conference of Asia, *Race and Minority Issues*, Singapore 1978, p. 13.
30. See Masao Maruyama's view in *Rekishi Ishiki No Kosō or* (Ancient Stratum in Japanese History Awareness).
31. School of Theology, Doshisha University, Kyoto, Japan, *Church Labor Letter* 140, August 1978.
32. *Critical Issues in Modern Religion*, p. 186.
33. Ibid., p. 446.
34. The Pali Text Society, *Dialogues of the Buddha*, vol. II, 1910, pp. 173, 176.
35. Karl Marx, *Capital*, Glaisher, London 1912, vol. I, p. 230.
36. Article on 'Adam' in *The Interpreter's Dictionary of the Bible*, Abingdon Press 1962, vol. 1, p. 42.
37. *Suffering and Hope*, An Anthology of Asian Writings, Christian Conference of Asia 1976, p. 19.
38. Rudolf Otto, *The Idea of the Holy*, reissued Oxford University Press 1968.
39. *The Uppsala 68 Report*, World Council of Churches, Geneva 1968, p. 241.
40. Christian Conference of Asia, *Workbook on Race and Minority Issues*, p. 26.
41. WCC, 'Racism in Churches', p. 111.
42. WCC, 'Fundamental Convictions', pp. 109f.
43. V. T. Rajshekar Shetty, *Crocodile Tears over Harijan Atrocities*, Dalit Action Committee, Bangalore 1978, p. 5.
44. B. R. Ambedkar, *Mr Gandhi and the Emancipation of Untouchables*, Bhim Patrika Publication, Jullundum, India 1943, p. 11.
45. D. J. Elwood (ed.), *What Asian Christians are Thinking*, New Day Publishers, Manila 1976, p. 260.
46. Rene Dubos, *A God Within*, Scribners, New York 1972, p. 202.
47. Ibid., p. 204.